Depression
Anxiety Therapy

Free Your Mind, Cognitive Behavioral Therapy And Other Proven Techniques To Guide Yourself Out Of Negative Thoughts.

Matthew Wright

By reading this document, the reader agrees that under no circumstances is the author responsible for any losses, direct or indirect, which are incurred as a result of the use of the information contained within this document, including, but not limited to, errors, omissions, or inaccuracies.

Table of Contents

Introduction

Depression is a disorder that makes someone feel sad or moody, and it affects how one thinks as well as how they associate with people. The way one behaves when they feel depressed can lead to emotional as well as physical issues. You are affected by how you do your activities and also do not appreciate what life has given you. Depression makes one feel weak, and you need to undergo treatment as well as therapies. Depression makes one thinks that nobody cares nor loves them. When you have depression symptoms that have lasted for two weeks that is when you can be termed to have depression. There are different types of depressions depending on circumstances or the period it has lasted.

Feeling hopeless, lack of appetite, difficulties in sleeping as well as feeling helpless are signs and symptoms of depression. When undergoing depression, one may have suicidal thoughts and even go to the extent of attempting to commit suicide. Different people have different signs and symptoms of depression. Some may have several symptoms, while others undergo many. The stage of grief may as well determine the intensity of symptoms. It can affect anyone regardless of their age, but more often, it is witnessed in adults. Depression, when intense, is followed by other medical cases. When not treated, it can lead to numerous risk factors. Depression is treatable even if it is a severe case, but it is more effective to treat it at an early stage. Either taking antidepressants or therapies can manage it, and in some cases, both the methods are applicable. If a depressed patient does not respond positively to the treatment, they should be electroconvulsive as well as any given therapy that will stimulate the brain.

Depression can be treated using various types of antidepressants. They boost how your brain makes use of a specific chemical to put your mood as well as stress under control. Getting an antidepressant that will work best for you will require you to try several and see the one with bearable side effects. Most preferably, you can consider using an antidepressant that a family member with depression has ever used. You need to consult your doctor when to stop taking the antidepressants. In cases where one feels better then decides to stop taking the medication without consulting the doctor, the depression is likely to return. Withdrawal symptoms can hit you once you stop the drug abruptly, but instead, you need the help of a doctor to decrease your dosage slowly and safely.

Persons under the age of twenty-five tend to have more suicidal thoughts when undergoing treatment. It is the case in the first weeks under antidepressants or dosage change, and for that, they need to be taken care of. Persons of all ages are likely to experience this in the first weeks of antidepressant administration. It is advisable to make an appointment with your doctor if you suspect you may be suffering from depression.

Chapter 1 What Is Cognitive Behavioral Therapy

What Constitutes Cognitive Behavioral Therapy?

CBT is a psychotherapeutic methodology that means to show an individual new aptitude on the best method to take care of issues concerning useless feelings, practices, and insights through an objective situated, efficient methodology. This title is utilized from numerous points of view to separate behavioral therapy, cognitive therapy, and therapy that depends on both social and cognitive therapy. There is an experimental proof that demonstrates that CBT is very successful in treating a few conditions, including psychotic disorders, temperament, anxiety, personality, substance misuse, and mood. Treatment is regularly manualized, as explicit mental requests are treated with explicit method driven brief, direct, and time-constrained medications.

Perhaps the best challenge is precisely characterizing what a subjective social treatment is. The specific helpful strategies fluctuate inside the various methodologies of CBT relying on what sort of issues are being managed, yet the techniques typically revolve around the following:

- Keeping a diary of important occasions and related sentiments, behaviors, and contemplations.

- Questioning and testing perceptions, assessments, presumptions, and convictions that may be ridiculous and unhelpful.

- It is gradually confronting exercises that may have been kept away from.

- We are trying out better approaches for carrying on and responding.

What's more, interruption procedures, care, and unwinding are additionally ordinarily utilized in CBT. Mind-set balancing out prescriptions is likewise frequently joined with treatments to treat conditions like the bipolar issue. CBT is applied to a wide range of circumstances, including the accompanying conditions:

- Anxiety issue (over the top impulsive issue, social fear or social tension, summed up nervousness issue)

- Mood issue (clinical misery, significant burdensome issue, mental indications)

- Insomnia (counting being more powerful than the medication Zopiclone)

- Severe mental issue (schizophrenia, bipolar issue, serious depression)

- Children and young people (significant burdensome issue, tension issue, injury and posttraumatic stress issue side effects)

- Stuttering (to enable them to beat uneasiness, shirking practices, and negative contemplations about themselves)

CBT includes showing an individual new ability to conquer useless feelings, practices, and insights through an objective situated, efficient methodology. There is observational proof demonstrating that intellectual, behavioral therapy is viable in treating numerous conditions, including fanatical urgent issue, summed up uneasiness issue, significant burdensome issue, schizophrenia, nervousness, and negative contemplations about oneself). With the tremendous measure of progress appeared by the utilization of this treatment, it is one of the most significant devices that analysts and advisors need to treat mental issue today.

Nonetheless, most CBT has the accompanying attributes:

1. **CBT depends on the Cognitive Model of Emotional Response.**

CBT depends on the possibility that our contemplations cause our emotions and practices, not outer things, similar to individuals, circumstances, and occasions. The advantage of this reality is that we can change how we think to feel/act better regardless of whether the circumstance doesn't change.

2. **CBT is shorter and Time-Limited.**

CBT is considered among the quickest regarding outcomes acquired. The normal number of sessions clients get (over a wide range of issues and ways to deal with CBT) is just 16. Different types of therapy, similar to psychoanalysis, can take years. What empowers CBT to be briefer is its profoundly informative nature and the way that it utilizes schoolwork assignments. CBT is time-constrained in that we help clients comprehend at the earliest reference point of the treatment procedure that there will be a moment that the proper treatment will end. The ending of proper therapy is a choice made by the client and therapy. Accordingly, CBT isn't an open-ended, ceaseless procedure.

3. **A sound remedial relationship is important for powerful treatment, however not the core interest.**

A few types of treatment expect that the primary explanation individuals show signs of improvement in treatment is a direct result of the positive connection between the advisor and client. CBTs trust it is critical to have a decent, confiding relationship. However, that isn't sufficient. CBT specialists accept that the clients change since they figure out how to think distinctively, and they follow up on that learning. In this way, CBTs center around showing sound self-directing aptitudes.

4. **CBT is a collective exertion between the specialist and the client.**

Intellectual, social advisors, look to realize what their clients truly desire (their objectives), and after that help, their clients accomplish those objectives. The specialist's job is to tune in, instruct, and empower, while the client's jobs are to express concerns, learn, and execute that learning.

5. CBT depends on the unemotional way of thinking.

Not all ways to deal with CBT underscore aloofness. Reasonable Emotive Behavior Therapy, Rational Behavior Therapy, and Rational Living Therapy underline apathy. Beck's Cognitive Therapy did not depend on aloofness. Psychological, social treatment doesn't tell individuals how they should feel. Nonetheless, the vast majority looking for treatment would prefer not to feel the way they have been feeling. The methodologies that underscore emotionless shows the advantages of inclination, at the very least, quiet when stood up to with unwanted circumstances. They additionally accentuate the way that we have our bothersome circumstances, whether we are vexed about them or not. In the event that we are vexed about our issues, we have two issues - the issue, and our agitated about it. A great many people need to have the least number of issues conceivable. So when we figure out how to all the more tranquility acknowledge an individual issue, in addition to the fact that we feel better, yet we, for the most part, put ourselves in a superior situation to utilize our insight, information, vitality, and assets to determine the issue.

6. **CBT utilizes the Socratic Method.**

CBT needs to increase the excellent comprehension of its clients' worries. That is the reason they frequently pose inquiries. They additionally urge their clients to pose inquiries of themselves, similar to, "How would I truly realize that those individuals are snickering at me?" "Might they be able to chuckle about something different?"

7. **CBT is organized and directive.**

CBT has a particular motivation for every session. Explicit methods/ideas are educated during every session. CBT centers around the client's objectives. We don't tell our clients what their objectives "should" be, or what they "should" endure. We order as we tell our clients the best way to think and carry on in approaches to get what they need. Along these lines, CBT advisors don't guide their clients - rather, they show their clients how to do.

8. **CBT depends on an instructive model**.

CBT depends on the logically bolstered supposition that most enthusiastic and social responses are found out. Along these lines, the objective of treatment is to enable clients to unlearn their undesirable responses and to gain proficiency with another method for responding. Hence, CBT has nothing to do with "simply talking." Individuals can "simply talk" with anybody. The instructive accentuation of CBT has an extra advantage - it prompts long haul results. At the point when individuals see how and why they are getting along well, they realize what to do to keep progressing nicely.

9. **CBT hypothesis and strategies depend on the Inductive Method.**

A focal part of rational reasoning is that it depends on actuality. Frequently, we upset ourselves about things when the truth is told, and the circumstance isn't caring for what we think it is. On the off chance that we realized that, we would not burn through our time upsetting ourselves. In this way, the inductive technique urges us to take a gander at our considerations as being theories or speculations that can be addressed and tried. If we find that our speculations are mistaken (because we have new data), at that point, we can change our intuition to be by how the circumstance truly is.

10. **Homework is a focal component of CBT.**

If when you endeavored to get familiar with your duplication tables, you went through just a single hour of the week contemplating them, you may, in any case, be thinking about what 5 X 5 equivalents. You likely invested a lot of energy at home considering your augmentation tables, possibly with cheat sheets. The equivalent is the situation with psychotherapy. Objective accomplishment (whenever got) could take an exceptionally prolonged time if every individual were just to consider the methods and points educated was for one hour out of every week. That is the reason CBT specialists dole out understanding assignments and urge their clients to rehearse the procedures learned.

How Cognitive Behavior Therapy Works

CBT works by pinpointing musings that ceaselessly ascend, utilizing them as the sign for positive activity, and supplanting them with more beneficial, all the more enabling options.

The core of CBT is learning self-adapting aptitudes, enabling patients to deal with their responses/reactions to circumstances all the more skillfully, change the contemplations they let themselves know, and practice "sane self-directing." While it certainly helps for the CBT advisor/instructor and patient to fabricate trust and have a decent relationship, the power truly lies in the patient's hands.

How willing a patient is to investigate their considerations, remain liberal, complete schoolwork assignments, and practice persistence during the CBT procedure all decide how gainful CBT will be for them.

A portion of the qualities that make intellectual, behavioral therapy, special and powerful include:

•   **Rational approach:** CBT hypothesis and systems depend on level-headed reasoning, which means they intend to distinguish and utilize certainties. The "inductive technique" of CBT urges patients to look at their very own recognitions and convictions to check whether they are in actuality reasonable. In CBT, there is a fundamental supposition that most enthusiastic and social responses are found out. Commonly with a CBT specialist's assistance, patients discover that there since quite a while ago held presumptions and theories are in any event in part wrong, which causes them superfluous stressing and enduring.

•   **Law of entropy and fleetingness:** CBT lays on logical suspicions, including the law of entropy, which is the way that "on the off chance that you don't utilize it, you lose it." We generally can change how we feel because our sentiments are established in our minds' compound communications, which are always advancing. If we break cycles of idea designs, our minds will alter to improve things. X-ray outputs demonstrate the human mind makes and continues neural neurotransmitters (associations) between continuous contemplations and feelings, so if you practice positive reasoning, your cerebrum will make it simpler to feel more joyful later on.

• **Accepting terrible or agonizing feelings:** Many CBT advisors can enable patients to figure out how to remain quiet and sensible in any event, when they're looked with bothersome circumstances. Figuring out how to acknowledge troublesome contemplations or feelings as being "essentially some portion of life" is vital, even though this can help prevent an endless loop from shaping. Frequently we get resentful about our intense emotions and extra significantly all the more anguish. Rather than including self-fault, outrage, dissatisfaction, trouble, or frustration to effectively extreme emotions, CBT instructs patients to tranquility acknowledge an issue without judgment to not aggravate it even.

• **Questioning and communicating:** Cognitive conduct specialists, for the most part, ask patients numerous inquiries to enable them to increase another point of view, see the circumstance all the more unmistakably and sensibly, and help them covert how they truly feel.

- **Specific agendas and systems:** CBT is generally done in a progression of sessions that each have a particular objective, idea, or procedure to work with. In contrast to some different types of treatment, sessions are not just for the advisor and patient to talk straightforwardly without motivation at the top of the priority list. CBT specialists show their clients how to all the more likely handle troublesome musings and emotions by rehearsing explicit methods during sessions that can later be applied to life when they're generally required.

Chapter 2 Benefits of Cognitive-Behavioral Therapy

Ultimately, cognitive-behavioural therapy has several important benefits, all of which compound to make it so incredibly effective. These different benefits all work together, and the result is entirely undeniable—Cognitive-behavioural therapy has been so incredibly popular that even the United States military recognizes it as one of the best treatments for PTSD in patients.

The benefits and possibilities of cognitive-behavioural therapy are almost limitless, with several of these being distinctly unique to cognitive-behavioural therapy in the sense that cognitive-behavioural therapy can treat some problems without a need for prescription medication while still seeing a drastic improvement of symptoms. Of course, this book is not advocating that you should drop any medications that you are on without first speaking to your doctor—you should only make changes to your prescriptions and your medical regimen if you are seeking the advice of the medical professional who prescribed them in the first place.

If you have gotten this far and are currently debating whether cognitive-behavioural therapy could be good for you, rest assured that there are very few people who would not benefit from the process of cognitive-behavioural therapy and cognitive restructuring. Nearly anyone could stand to learn some of the key skills involved in the process of restructuring one's mind and how to set goals or go through the other steps that are integral to the cognitive-behavioural therapy process. However, if you are still relatively unconvinced, try taking a look at some of the following benefits that cognitive-behavioural therapy has to offer when it is completed:

Teaches to Identify Negative Thoughts

Cognitive-behavioural therapy makes it a point to teach patients how to identify negative thoughts. After all, negative thoughts are directly related to negative feelings and behaviours. By learning to identify negative thoughts, the individual can begin giving less stock to those negative thoughts, instead of reminding him or herself that those negative thoughts are unproductive and serve a little benefit to everyone involved. All those negative thoughts will do is ensure that the individual struggles further, creating negative feelings and behaviours.

When you can identify negative thoughts, however, you can stop them in their tracks with cognitive restructuring, a skill that will be introduced to you in-depth later within this book. When you engage in cognitive restructuring, you are essentially ensuring that you can control your thoughts and feelings on a specific subject, and when you gain that control over your thoughts and feelings, you gain control over your behaviour as well.

For example, you may have the negative thought of, "I am always so bad at everything I try." That negative thought then leads you never to try anything because you will be bad at everything you attempt, never mind the fact that most people are bad at most things they try for the first time. Skills take time to build, and that negative thought you have discouraged you from ever trying in the first place. Because you do not see the point in attempting to fix yourself or your thought, you end up stuck feeling as you can never learn anything new. That negative thought essentially cripples you, dissuading you from any personal growth that could be incredibly beneficial to you.

When you can identify that negative thought, however, you can begin to overcome it. You can remind yourself that the negative thought that is colouring your perceptions of reality and what is happening around you is not important to maintain and that you have no reason to hold yourself back from trying new things simply because you fear you may be bad at them. You can then remind yourself that it is normal to be bad at something at first and that you will get better the more you practice.

Prevents a Relapse of Addiction

People who have used cognitive-behavioural therapy for addiction oftentimes find that they are less likely to relapse. Because they have developed coping skills specific to their mindset and their belief systems, they are then able to ensure that they do not relapse. They can use their coping mechanisms any time the sudden urge for their drug of choice arises. In doing so, they protect themselves from negative behaviours, allowing them to heal and remain sober.

When the addict does not have these methods or has not gone through the process of learning to control his impulses, he is far more likely to relapse simply because talking through a problem or not developing any coping mechanisms, to begin with, will not keep the impulses from becoming overwhelming.

For example, if a patient started using their drug of choice after a particularly traumatic loss, a psychotherapist may try to talk through that loss in hopes of strengthening the individual and ensuring that he or she does not continue to use it. The problem is removed, and with resolving the problem, the idea is that the addict will no longer have the motivation to self-medicate. However, once the taste for the drug is there, they may tend to instead resort to that drug of choice any time there is a particularly stressful occurrence. Any time stress gets difficult; they relapse because there is a new trigger.

With cognitive-behavioural therapy, however, those new triggers are all managed the same way as the original one—with coping skills meant to be effective at destroying the motivation to use in the first place. Because cognitive-behavioural therapy focused on crushing impulses to use rather than the original root of the behaviour in the first place, the individual already has the skills lined up to fight off future impulses just as he has been.

Teaches Anger Management

Cognitive-behavioural therapy is also particularly relevant when it comes to anger management. Oftentimes, people with anger problems attempt to solve them but never really manage to make much of a dent. Cognitive-behavioural therapy, on the other hand, attempts to teach coping mechanisms for anger. As anger arises, the patient is capable of managing his or her emotions, recognizing when the anger is coming up and getting too powerful, and when he or she knows that the anger is going to come tumbling out, he or she can then cope with it somehow.

Frequently, this is effective because it manages the individual's ability to create changes. The individual can change his or her behaviours, creating better ones in their places and ensuring that he or she is capable of making the good choices necessary for everyone around them.

For example, if you have a problem with anger, you are likely taught first to identify the triggers for your anger. Note that these triggers are not the same as the root for your anger issues—they are the several stimuli that may trigger the emotional, angry reaction that you are hoping to overcome. Through teaching how best to overcome these emotional reactions, you develop the ability to utilize them and prevent major outbursts. You likely were taught several grounding mechanisms that will enable you to effectively and almost entirely control your emotional impulses. This is great—this means that your anger no longer gets the best of you, and you are capable of controlling yourself.

Helps Cope with Loss

People who suffer from a loss oftentimes struggle with grief for a long while after the loss. Especially when that loss is tragic, such as the loss of a child, the individual likely struggles to know how to cope. When grief becomes overwhelming, the individual struggles with how best to manage.

Grief oftentimes involves several negative feelings as the individual comes to terms with the fact that a loved one is lost. These feelings can range from sadness to guilt, anger tor resentment or regret, and the wide range of emotions can be almost debilitating if the individual does not know how best to cope with it.

This is where cognitive-behavioural therapy steps in—it can begin walking the individual suffering from loss through the process of learning to grieve effectively in a way that will not be detrimental to the functioning of the individual. By ensuring that the individual can grieve in his or her way while also dealing with teaching coping mechanisms for when the grief gets too bad, such as grounding techniques for when the feelings grow too overwhelming, cognitive-behavioural therapy encourages swifter healing. The cognitive-behavioural therapy model recognizes the fact that grief is not linear and that it is constantly changing and evolving as the individual changes and evolves—sometimes someone may be okay, and suddenly, years later, the grief slams back in his or her face.

Through the process of learning to cope with grief instead of guiding the patient through coping, the therapist can give the individual tools necessary to survive even when the guilt and grief made a surprise comeback when it was the least expected possibility. This creates a sort of strength and permanence in which the individual can grieve without feeling overwhelmed by the process. He can actively grieve while remaining largely functions as an individual, capable of working and functioning through the grief as expected beyond the first few weeks of losing someone dear to you.

Manages Pain without Medication

Those who are often in chronic pain find themselves frequently suffering from depression or anxiety as a nearly direct result. The constant pain can be crippling to someone, causing an onslaught of guilt in not being able to function as intended, discomfort at the physical pain, feelings of worthlessness that the individual's body is so incapable of normal life, and many other negative emotions. The individual suffering from this chronic pain, however, may be able to work out how to avoid the pain pills without having to suffer further.

Remember, cognitive-behavioural therapy sees the vast majority of actions and senses as neutral, with the thoughts being what skews something positive or negative. This is true for pain as well—when the pain is the problem that is making it difficult to function, cognitive-behavioural therapy can create all sorts of methods in which the individual can begin to cope. Cognitive-behavioural therapy may involve restructuring the thinking about pain being entirely negative, quite possibly including affirmations that remind the individual that some pain means the body is attempting to heal.

Particularly after surgery or some other highly physical event in which painkillers are needed, these sorts of affirmations and treatments could keep an individual off of painkillers if he or she was afraid of what would happen after using commonly prescribed narcotics for pain relief. The individual could instead choose to engage in cognitive-behavioural therapy techniques for coping with pain, in which the thoughts on the pain being felt are directly changed to something more productive, eliminating the negativity that surrounded the thought process and therefore enabling the individual to better cope with any negativity being felt.

Mitigating Effects of PTSD

People suffering from PTSD oftentimes find cognitive-behavioural therapy to be incredibly effective. Those who use cognitive-behavioural therapy find nearly permanent relief early on in the process. They can ensure that they manage to treat their issues without drugs, seeing a drastic decrease in debilitating symptoms. While they may still experience flashbacks or other symptoms sometimes, the individuals are well-equipped to handle the problem through their knowledge of various coping mechanisms.

When people can better cope with their PTSD, they turn to less destructive methods—they no longer need to attempt any sort of self-medication. They can better function in society, even if they have a particularly niche cause of their PTSD in the first place, such as a very specific accident in a common car, which has caused flashbacks and panic attacks to the sight of said common car. With the methods and coping mechanisms, the individual can better mitigate the panic attacks associated with the car. He can tell himself that the car is not worthy of concern and that the feelings are just anxiety and not an actual threat. In doing so, the individual can sort of conqueror the panic attack, ensuring it does not get bad enough to be debilitating.

Creating Resolutions for Relationships Issues

When there is trouble in paradise, couples oftentimes struggle to come to a consensus. There can be serious problems that arise in relationships, especially if neither party is particularly skilled at any sort of relationship management or conflict resolution. Luckily, cognitive-behavioural therapy can be helpful with both of those. Through cognitive-behavioural therapy, individuals can learn healthy conflict management skills, as well as skills necessary to control negative impulses and emotions to ensure that the relationship can continue healthily. Through the process of cognitive-behavioural therapy, both people can identify the problems that they have, identify where the flawed thought process is, and how best to solve the problems at hand without conflict.

For example, if one person is particularly nervous about relationships and conflict because of prior experience being cheated on, causing her to be incredibly jealous and possessive in the relationship, several methods can help mitigate the problem. The individual can create some self-worth affirming affirmations to repeat to remind her that she is worthy of love and respect, even if she may feel like she is not sometimes. She can then develop any of the skills needed to ensure that she can control her impulses, especially since her emotional impulses tend to guide her in the wrong direction. She learns how to use grounding techniques to prevent herself from getting too worked up over situations at hand, and that enables her to instead focus on her emotional management. In doing so, she can stop and calmly and rationally discuss her feelings with her partner to come to a legitimate solution.

Effective
As you can see with the myriad of examples that have been provided within this chapter, the effects of cognitive-

behavioural therapy are essentially limitless. The sky is the limit, and cognitive-behavioural therapy can help in nearly anything that is caused by a relationship between thoughts, emotions, and behaviours, which is essentially the entirety of human behaviour.

The effects are not only relatively quickly acting, but they are also nearly permanent—once someone has learned a skill, it can be reused and repurposed nearly limitlessly, with no need for further therapy or guidance. Once the individual has mastered a skill, it is free to use from then on, creating the perfect opportunity for the individual to manage other difficult situations.

Because cognitive-behavioural therapy is so focused on the teaching of important skills that can be used, it can create the unique result of creating nearly permanent results. Several other therapies and medications see a relapse of destructive thoughts or behaviours shortly after the cessation of treatment, but that does not happen with cognitive-behavioural therapy. CBT is so focused on skills that it bypasses the entire issue of relapse, creating a more effective antidepressant that costs less because it requires fewer sessions.

Overall, not only does cognitive-behavioural therapy tout the best results in the least amount of time, but it is also a nearly permanent fix, making it the most cost-effective of the methods to treat a wide range of the conditions cognitive-behavioural therapy can tackle. With all of these different benefits, you may be wondering what the downside is—the answer is that you may experience some mental distress, particularly when dealing with difficult topics and concepts, but by and large, you can get through the process with very little risk and discomfort. Aside from feeling uncomfortable as you parse through some of the more difficult subject matter, you are not likely to face any serious side effects in the way that you would with, say, medication, for example. The process is quite straightforward, and the only risk is upset feelings as you deal with the process of learning new coping mechanisms.

Chapter 3 A Brief History of Cognitive Behavioral Therapy

Cognitive Behavioral Therapy (CBT) is a methodology utilized by psychotherapists to impact a patient's emotions and behaviors. The way to the methodology is in its technique, which must be efficient. It has been effectively utilized to treat an assortment of clutters, including dietary issues, substance misuse, anxiety, and character issue. It tends to be utilized in individual or gathering treatment sessions, and the methodology can likewise be outfitted towards self-improvement treatment.

CBT is a mix of customary behavioral therapy and cognitive therapy. They are consolidated into a therapy that is centered around indication expulsion. The ampleness of the treatment can undeniably be settled on a choice about the subject to its results. The more it is used, the more it has advanced toward getting to be proposed. It is currently utilized as the main treatment procedure for posttraumatic stress disorder, bulimia, obsessive-compulsive disorder, and depression. CBT initially started to be utilized somewhere in the range of 1960 and 1970. It was a progressive procedure for combining cognitive therapy techniques and behavioral therapy techniques. Behavioral therapy had been existing prior to the early 1930s, yet cognitive therapy was not made known until the 1960s. Notable advantages of consolidating it with social treatment procedures were figured out. Ivan Pavlov, with his canines who salivated at the ringing of the supper ringer, was among the most well-known of the conduct research pioneers. Different pioneers in the field included Clark Hull and John Watson.

Rather than concentrating on examining the issue like Freud and the psychoanalysts, CBT concentrated on disposing of the indications. The thought whenever you take out the manifestations, you have disposed of the issue. This more straightforward methodology was viewed as progressively powerful at getting to the present issue and assisting patients to gain ground all the more speedily. As a gradually radical dynamic treatment, conduct procedures managed increasingly extreme issues. The more evident and clearer cut the side effects were, the simpler it was to target them and devise medications to dispose of them. Behavioral therapy was not as effective at first with increasingly vague issues, for example, depression. This domain was better off with cognitive therapy strategies.

In numerous scholastic settings, the two therapy methods were utilized one next to the other to look into the results. On different occasions, the benefits of combining the two systems turned out to be clear as a technique for exploiting the qualities of each. David Barlow's research on frenzy issue medicines gave the principal a solid case of the accomplishment of the consolidated techniques.

Chapter 4 A Closer Look at Anxiety and Depression

To get a better understanding of how CBT works, we must get a clearer understanding of how our mind works in general. When we have thoughts, they usually fly through our minds in a tiny fraction of a second; quite often we don't even realize that we've had a thought, let alone the effects it has on our behavior.

So, when you lose a loved one in death, lose your job, deal with a family break-up, or have some other traumatic situation, you are quite likely to feel some level of sadness or even fear about what's in store for your future. These are pretty normal reactions to devastating events in our lives. We don't realize that these feelings and the behaviors that follow are a direct result of our thoughts. Most people will bounce back in time and get back to living life. However, for some, these low emotional states tend to be more intense and can linger for extended periods.

What is depression?

Depression, which tends to occur more in women than in men, is the direct result of these lingering thoughts. The way it manifests itself can vary depending on a person's age and gender. In men, it may be seen in symptoms such as tiredness, irritability, and sometimes anger. Men tend to behave more recklessly when they are depressed, which can be seen by their abuse of drugs or alcohol. These behaviors may often be passed off as masculine, so they are less likely to recognize it as depression and are not inclined to seek help or treatment.

Women in a depressed state are more likely to appear sad and have deep feelings of worthlessness and guilt. They may be reluctant to take part in social activities or engage with others, even those who are close to them. Depression in children will also be different. Young children may refuse to go to school or show signs of separation anxiety when parents leave. Teenagers are more likely to be irritable, sulky, and often get into trouble in school. In more extreme cases, you might see signs of an eating disorder or substance abuse.

What is anxiety?

Closely associated with depression is anxiety, which can manifest itself in a variety of ways. A mild case of anxiety might be evidenced by the sensation of butterflies in the stomach in anticipation of an important event, concern about meeting deadlines, or nervousness about an anticipated treatment or procedure.

For most people, when anxiety is present, they can just ride it out. It is a normal part of life. However, some types of anxiety that are far from the norm. Some anxieties can trigger fears (spiders, snakes, planes, etc.) or phobias that are excessive and irrational. Many people have a fear of snakes even though they have never actually come in contact with one. Others are afraid of dogs even though they have never had a bad experience with one. This type of anxiety easily develops into an anxiety disorder.

To help in differentiating between normal anxiety and an anxiety disorder, first, take a close look at the cause of the anxiety. Then look at the instinctive response to that fear. If the behavior is considered realistic, then it is probably 'normal' anxiety. However, if the response is viewed as extreme enough to disrupt normal life, it could be classified as an anxiety disorder.

For example, you may be anxious about getting sick, so you take steps to prevent illness. You may use hand sanitizer, regularly wash your hands, or even avoid shaking hands with people in public places. This is a normal form of anxiety. On the other hand, if your fear of getting sick is so strong that you don't want to leave your home or you are constantly washing and cleaning, you may have an anxiety disorder.

There are many different types of anxiety-related disorders out there, and for your convenience, these disorders have been grouped into three different categories:

- Anxiety disorders

Excessive fear of a real or perceived threat

- Obsessive-compulsive disorders

Intrusive fearful thoughts that trigger compulsive behaviors

- Trauma/stressor-related disorders

The extreme reaction to a past traumatic or stress-related event

If you suspect you or someone you know has an anxiety disorder and is struggling to overcome the symptoms, CBT is one way to help. This method of helping patients identify the thought process that triggers the fear may be the best solution to the problem.

The Causes of depressions

The faulty mood causes this disorder. The emotion is about the general feeling one has about a specific event or a person. This aspect can also be called as an attitude or the public emotions people have. Moods can be positive or negative. Some positive moods include joy, happiness, a feeling of self-worthiness, and many others. However, when considering depression, it is associated with bad attitudes, which involves one being sad, anxious, low self-esteem, anger, narcissistic, arrogance, and many other emotions.

Other specialists believe this menace originates from the genes. They say that like 'father like son. Therefore, if the parent experiences some personality disorder, the offspring is likely to experience the same jeopardy. Some studies show that if your twin is depressed, there is a high percentage that you will experience the same illness. People of similar genetic makeup show similar vulnerabilities if especially the people are angry. They are likely to experience some mood swings and unstable emotions that lead to stress.

Another cause is drug abuse in some people. Some individuals take hard drugs that affect their mentality. Such personnel may change from a happy individual to a stressed character. Some medications have impacts like hallucinations, sedation, stimulation, and other effects that increase their anxiety and personality disorders. Hence such fellows will anticipate an illusion and unrealistic goals if otherwise they are not attained thy quickly get depressed. Intoxication affects your rational beliefs and values and makes you moody, such that you are stressed due to less irritation.

Some medical conditions, like chronic diseases, put one under trauma. Such illness has painful ordeals and events. Moreover, they cause stigma to your beloved ones. Therefore, the victims view themselves as a deadweight to the family where the end-results are losing their self-esteem and feeling miserable. If you have a chronic disease like stroke, you will think others are doing more for you, which is unnecessary. Therefore, you will likely feel heartened and stressed. Consequently, one will be miserable and hopeless.

The environmental conditions that surround you may lead to distress. Imagine being surrounded by assaultive parents, poverty conditions, or your family is regarded as an outcast. That atmosphere you are living in makes one feel unappreciated. Some instances of early childhood trauma can cause depression. Take a situation a child being assaulted, that scar will probably remain with him or her for the rest of their lives.

What are the Symptoms of Depression?

The number one symptom of depression that most people recognize is the feeling of overwhelming, uncontrollable sadness or having a depressed mood. Sometimes, the individual may not be able to describe their depression as sadness but may instead describe it as feeling "nothingness." This, too, can be a sign that depression is at play and that the person is struggling with symptoms of depression.

Another big sign of someone struggling with depression is feeling disinterested in things that used to be pleasurable or enjoyable for them. Or, if the depression is, further along, feeling disinterested in doing anything at all. Some people who are struggling with more advanced or severe forms of depression may struggle to even take care of their basic needs like brushing their teeth, getting enough nutrition, or getting to work daily.

In addition to struggling with taking care of themselves, they may find that they have an irregular sleep cycle and an irregular appetite. A person with depression may sleep too much, or struggle to sleep at all. Likewise, they might eat too much, or struggle to eat at all. They may also find themselves losing energy in general or constantly feeling fatigued even if they are not tired enough to sleep.

Physically, a person who is struggling with depression may find their movements slowing down and may find themselves struggling with staying active. They may physically walk or move slower, talk slower, or generally behave slower compared to usual. This may not be as recognizable to them as it is to others, although they may feel on some level that they are moving slower and they may think it's just due to tiredness.

In their minds, people with depression often experience thoughts of being worthless or guilty about something, even when they have nothing to be guilty about. They may feel guilty that their lack of motivation and energy is hurting the people around them, even if it isn't, because of their distorted perception of reality. They may also have difficulty thinking, as well as difficulty concentrating, and making decisions may be too challenging for them. In some cases, people with depression may also think or feel suicidal or have frequent thoughts of death to the point where they romanticize death in their minds.

To be classified as clinical depression, a person must have these symptoms for at least two weeks. However, if you have symptoms associated with suicidal thoughts or death, this is a strong sign that you are dealing with depression, and you should not wait for a diagnosis to seek and begin treatment.

Types of Depressions

Depression occurs in diverse, which means it occurs in very many ways. Being anxious or having unstable emotions are some of the renowned personality disorders. Imagine the emotional impact one gets after watching your loved one feeling depressed. It is, therefore, a hurtful situation. The consequences are destructive, which can even result in the individual committing suicide.

For a proper treatment of such victims, it is wise to know the type of depression one is experiencing. It is advisable to visit a clinic as soon as you realize you are experiencing some sorrows disorders. Visit the therapist as early as possible because depression is manageable at an early stage. When it is at its late-stage, it develops to become a chronic condition that puts one under pressure of health complications. Recognizing the type of depression, you are suffering from is essential because the psychiatrist will know the kind of therapeutically program to put you through. The following are some of the types of this illness.

The first type is a major depressive disorder. It is a commonly known type of depression because it affects many people in society. It exhibits the typical symptoms that are accustomed to stressful reactions. These emotions involve the feeling of sadness, hopelessness, emptiness, low self-esteem, and loss of interest in major recreational activities. These symptoms are easily recognizable to a patient, and one should seek medical attention as early as possible. This disorder falls under two main categories, which are atypical depression and, melancholic type. The atypical ones always anxious therefore they eat and sleep a lot, and the melancholic beings tend to suffer from insomnia and guiltiness.

There is this type of stress which is resistant the antidepressant drugs. This kind of condition is referred to as the treatment of resistant depression. You can administer any medications to this patient, but still, they are not working. They always have unknown causes where their most prominent suspects are the genetic, or environmental causatives. For one to treat those victims, psychotherapy is recommended for one to assess the reason for that moody feeling. You may also administer different types of antidepressants to establish the medicine that heals that person.

Other people who are not healed quickly from significant depression experience the subsyndromal condition. This menace involves one experiencing many melancholic disorders. In simple one is engrossed with different symptoms showing varying characteristics. You may experience melancholic and at the same time, atypical illness. The physician must be quick to detect this condition because if the patient is affected by many sicknesses, chances of healing are less.

The persistent depressive disorder involves a state of stubborn symptoms. What does it mean by them being stubborn? It means that the syndrome is continuous over time. The syndromes seem to restructure themselves where if one sign is treated, it changes and reforms to terminal disorder. Such complications involve sleeping problems, fatigue, loss of appetite, and many other conditions. The best thing for a psychiatrist to diagnose such a patient is by combining both psychotherapy and medicinal diagnosis.

Depression due to diseases is another type. Some of the chronic illnesses cause stigma to the victims. Think of how you would react if tested HIV positive, cancer, or any other fatal diseases. 'I will kill myself,' 'everybody will laugh at me and despise me.' These are your probable thoughts you would experience if told the bad news. Feelings of loneliness, regret, and guiltiness will eat you strike on you like a hungry lion.

Substance intake depression is a major one attributed to the intoxicants. Intoxication comes from people indulging in drugs and alcohol. The results were those people hallucinating or do unusual things. They will, therefore, find other people do not agree to those deeds, hence they feel emotionally discouraged. Some end up in crimes and theft to buy those drugs. These substances change your mood, loss of concern on pleasurable practices, and feeling empty always. Specialized rehab centers are useful in healing those patients.

Dysthymia

This is a type of depression that is common amongst teens, although, adults also suffer dysthymia. Its symptoms are fewer than the other types of depression and must be confirmed by a physician before commencing treatments. One major thing about dysthymia is that it only lasts for not more than a year for children and teens between the ages of 13 to 18. It is estimated that 11% of teens in this age bracket suffer dysthymia over a lifetime.

Even though dysthymia is not considered as severe depression, it still poses some threats to the individual and should not be ignored. When dysthymia happens to adults, it lasts for two years and this is enough to cause a major episode in the adult. Generally, dysthymia is known as a low-grade depression, this is why a lot of people don't give it as much attention as they do other clinical types of depression. Dysthymia can also occur with clinical depression thereby lasting over two years for adults. When that happens, it is described as "Persistent Depressive Disorder." At this time, the individual has shifted from what would have been considered a minor depression to a more serious case of depression, leaving the individual at a greater risk than before. This is why people with dysthymia should always be looked out for as they tend to plunge into major depression.

People often make the mistake of concluding that those who are depressed or those going through clinical depression and have attempted suicide are weak. Depression as a health condition is not easy to deal with by the individual alone and most times the individual needs the support of loved ones and a professional to get through it. Some hold the belief that depression is a question of some defects, this is one of the myths surrounding the mental health condition. It may be the reason why it doesn't get the needed attention it deserves in some parts of the world. It has nothing to do with personal weakness, defects and also has nothing to do with a person's age, nationality or color. However, some other health conditions might send an individual into depression. Both males and females, old and young are at the risk of depression. As stated before, ignorance has allowed minor depression to grow into more severe clinical depression. This ignorance is sometimes on the part of the individual and sometimes from the society or environment the individual finds himself at the time.

Postnatal Depression

Even though there are different means a mother can give birth that will make it less painful and stressful, childbirth comes with its pains that sometimes lead to depression for the mother. This is known as "baby blue."

Post-natal depression, as the name implies, occurs after childbirth. In some cases, it passes after some days or even less than a day, but in other cases, it could strike as a major health issue. Some doctors might advise the mother not to go through pregnancy and childbirth again for her health. We have seen mothers plunge into depression after childbirth and eventually die leaving behind the baby and maybe a father. As you may already know, the overall health of a baby after birth oftentimes depends on the health of the mother. We are not just talking about physical health, but how stable the mother is emotionally, socially and mentally. If she's sick in any of these areas, it would most likely mal her overall sense of judgment which may not be ideal for the baby.

It is every parent's joy to have a baby. However, did you know that for some people, child giving can be stressful? Probably this amazes you, but it is a fact. Some mothers change their attitude after giving birth because there is a change in hormones, fatigue, or fear of raising a child. Fathers, in their part, can change their mood when they feel their workload will be increased. Consequently, some folks become stressful.

How CBT can help

By mastering the techniques in CBT, those with anxiety or depressive disorders can learn how to control those fears and the behaviours they trigger. The program will help to establish clear-cut goals to work on, teach them how to identify the thoughts that start the process and arm them with defense mechanisms to fight these behaviours.

CBT helps by providing completely new ways to process those thoughts, feelings, and behaviours, so the patients can better cope with these normal events that happen in life. Instead of reacting negatively to traumatic events, it gives them the ability to reframe the triggering event and experience it from an entirely new perspective.

CBT helps depression the same way it helps with any thought-based or thought-involved ailment: it teaches you how to regain control over your mind and direct your thoughts purposefully, intentionally, and in a way that supports your wellbeing. CBT is going to support you in healing your depression by helping you identify false and negative thoughts and intentionally replace them with healthier and more realistic ones. By being able to regain control over your thoughts, you will find yourself experiencing less depression because you will be perceiving and experiencing the world in a way that is less likely to lead to depression.

Remember that in CBT, the basis for emotional creation is perceived as being a five-step process: experience, perceive, think, believe, and feel. For depression, it is believed that the experiences you are having are leading to you to perceive the world in a depressed manner, which leads to thoughts and beliefs that support the development of depression. From there, you begin to experience feelings and emotions relating to depression, which can lead to continuous depression if you are consistently experiencing these same habitual cycles of experiencing, perceiving, thinking, believing, and feeling about your world.

When it comes to life, you are unlikely to be able to change your experiences. While you can have some control over what you experience, in many cases, a large part of our external world is unchangeable, and we will continue to experience it over and over again regardless of what we attempt to create, experience, or achieve. If you want to experience a massive change in your life, you need to focus more on your perception, your thoughts, and your beliefs so that you can intentionally create a mindset that supports you in having feelings that are not depression.

The way CBT works specifically is by building skills such as redirecting your thoughts, distracting yourself, developing resiliency, and intentionally increasing your motivation so that you can begin to take back control over your thought processes. This way, you can rewire your automatic perceptions around your experiences and begin to experience something more intentional and supportive of healthier thoughts and beliefs. As you continue to increase and use these skills, you will find yourself experiencing a far greater capacity to enjoy healthier feelings, too.

Learning how to interrupt and change automatic perceptions, thoughts, and beliefs is not entirely easy, so you must understand this and be gentle with yourself throughout the process. You need to understand that your brain works automatically in many ways and that attempting to change your automatic thoughts and behaviours can be challenging since you are trying to change your subconscious mind at that point.

As you continue engaging in CBT, you will find yourself beginning to regain intentional and mindful control over your thoughts around certain things in your life, which means that you will have an easier time changing your thoughts. Before you know it, you will find yourself experiencing freedom from your painful perceptions, thoughts, and beliefs, and you will find yourself moving toward healthier emotions as a result. The important takeaway from this is that even if you feel like you are not experiencing any changes, or if you are struggling to implement these changes, you need to continue committing to this change in your thought experiences. The more that you can continue practicing this, the more your commitment is going to contribute to you experiencing overall changes in your thoughts and beliefs. As a result, you will find yourself experiencing changes in your feelings and behaviours, too.

Chapter 5 The Multimodal Model (MMT)

Multimodal Therapy

One of the most comprehensive ways that people can use cognitive behavioural therapy is through Multimodal therapy. This is a type of therapy that utilizes several different avenues to allow people to see the different ways that they are affected by their anxiety and depression. Once they figure out how their anxiety or depression shapes each of these areas of their lives, they can begin working on the healing process and making sure that they can overcome the problems that they have. Multimodal is the way that a person's behaviour, affects, sensations, images, cognition, interpersonal relationships, and dependence are all affected by anxiety or depression.

Behaviour

The behaviour that is seen in people who have anxiety and/or depression is different depending on what they are dealing with and to what degree. It is important to note that many different behaviour problems can come from both anxiety and depression. These include:

Childish acts

Inappropriate acts

Extreme obedience

Destructive behaviour

Compulsive behaviour

High levels of self-control

While all of these behaviours are not uncommon to see in people who are not dealing with anxiety and depression, they can be exacerbated by the disorders. The main characteristic of this is that the behaviours are negative and can cause serious problems for the person who is doing the behaviours.

The multimodal way of treating these behaviours is to figure out what they are and directly address them to figure out what type of problems they could be caused as a secondary result of the disorders that are affecting the brain.

Affects

There is always a way that anxiety and depression can affect a person but when dealing with a multimodal type of treatment, the effect is the intensity of which emotions are felt, and actions are done. A person who has anxiety may have a much more intense effect than someone who has depression, and it can be a problem in both instances.

In general, someone who does not have a mental disorder would not generally feel very strong emotions. The emotions that people who have anxiety and depression feel are what can cause them to seek out therapy in the first place – they may be concerned that their emotions are out of control.

It is important to note that just recognizing these emotions and even, in some instances, talking about them, will not be able to change the way that they are in the brain. It is something that takes several levels of therapy to get to and can sometimes take a longer time to be able to address it. Different emotions are associated with the intensity, and that can change the way that the person who has anxiety or depression does things.

<u>Sensations</u>

These are the physical symptoms that are felt during a bout of anxiety or depression. The most common are:

Sweating

Tension

Physical pain

Nausea

Increased heart rate

Shaking

Fidgeting

These are common during an anxiety attack or even during a dark time while someone is depressed. They can affect the way that a person does things and it can be harder for a person to concentrate when these physical symptoms are going on.

The multimodal aspect of this is that one of the other things that are happening – like images or cognition – can cause each of these physical symptoms to manifest. Sometimes, though, there are problems and a person may feel these for no reason at all. They may not know it, but there could have been something that did trigger them to feel these feelings.

It is important to note that the sensations are not going to be fixed by fighting them. The person who feels the sensations should accept them for what they are because trying to fight them can make them worse. By acceptance, a person will be able to start the healing process that goes along with the therapy.

Images

People who have anxiety and depression are often able to see the worst possible scenario of a situation. This is imagery by which they associate nearly everything, and it can be a problem or a benefit. If someone is constantly thinking about the worst-case scenario, they may avoid doing simple things like driving or going to the store. This leads to even higher anxiety and depression levels for that person.

How images can be the good thing is that once someone learns to channel the imagery in their mind and turn it into a positive thing, it can help them to solve problems. It is not uncommon for creative people to be depressed or have anxiety because of the bold images that they often see.

Cognition

Self-talk and the inner voice are the easiest ways to understand cognition in any person. A person with anxiety or depression will often use negative self-talk, and they will have an inner voice that is not very strong. They may struggle with the thoughts that they do have or even their opinions of themselves.

When using multimodal therapy, the point is to try to replace the negative cognition with positive. This is done through various methods including using images to make things more positive for the person who is experiencing negative self-talk.

Interpersonal

There are many relationship issues that people may experience when they have anxiety or depression. It is something that can hurt the way that things are done and the way that they interact. With multimodal therapy, a person can change their interpersonal relationships by learning how to cope with things in a healthy way instead of being codependent to another person.

Dependence

When it comes to people who have anxiety or depression, there is a higher chance that they will have dependencies on chemicals or emotions. It can affect the way a person chooses to do things, but it can be different depending on the way that a person functions. Whether they can sleep, use drugs or even depend on another person will all be related to anxiety and depression. Multimodal therapy can change this by creating different cognitive patterns and negative associations with the dependency items. It is something that will change the way that the person can function and make them better able to deal with things without reaching for something that they had previously been dependent on.

The main idea of multimodal therapy is to combine each of the different aspects of negative thinking and negative behaviours and replace them with positive things. It is important that the person doing this does it in all areas and pays close attention to the way that each of the different aspects is connected.

Chapter 6 Rational Emotive Behavior Therapy Method (REBT)

This chapter examines rational emotive behavior therapy (REBT), how REBT works, the main belief that is consistent and relevant to REBT, the goals that defined rational emotive behavior (REB), and subsequently the models of REBT. In conclusion, the chapter discusses how you can recognize irrational thought patterns that you may be experiencing.

Defining Rational Emotive Behavior Therapy

Formerly known as rational therapy, rational emotive behavior therapy (REBT) is psychoanalysis that is based on empirical undertakings that are designed to help you overcome emotional, social complications, and interferences. As a result, enabling you to live a happy and positive life. By now, you should have realized that depression and anxiety disorders are elements that limit your capacity to live a fulfilling life due to the significant setbacks that they bring into your life. In this regard, REBT engages you to determine self-defeating and unproductive thoughts or feelings that you possess, challenge the rationality of these attitudes, and replace them with constructive ideas that are healthier for your wellbeing. American therapist developed REBT in the mid-1950s. Various theoretical assumptions govern REBT, and they include:

1. Human beings do not develop emotional disturbances due to the experiences that they encounter, but it is because of the negative thoughts and feelings that they create in response to such situations. In this sense, it is not an activity or a triggering event that produces emotional turmoil, but it is as a result of what you decide to believe about the adversity that causes you to develop dysfunctional emotions.

2. The second assumption is based on the innate nature of human beings to possess both irrational and rational tendencies. In this regard, the rational-

emotive leanings come from positive meaning you have about life, social constructivism, and self-confidence while the irrational emotive leanings develop through self-defeating and social destruction inclinations. It is the irrational leanings that overwhelm rational tendencies in the case of people who suffer from depression and anxiety disorders.

3. The third assumption in REBT is that the emotional aptitude of human beings through their thinking and action is never experienced in a transparent process but rather are overlapping entities. For instance, behaviors and emotions affect how we think, and how we feel similarly affects how we behave and react to things.

You should know that REBT is quite different when compared to the psychoanalysis approach. Now, this is because, psychoanalysis is founded on altering existing philosophical thinking and emotive behaviors in relation to yourself and others, while REBT places more emphasis on exploring the past to help you change the current emotive response that you have developed. This is why the REBT approach is mainly recommended for treating depression and anxiety since it enables you to explore your past and change your current thought processes from irrational thinking to rational, healthier thought processes. Furthermore, the general teachings ingrained in REBT is that in the vent that you turn flexible preferences into grandiose, then such an undertaking inclines you to get emotionally disturbed and upset.

How Rational Emotive Behavior Therapy Works

Based on the assumption that people tend to blame their irrational and destructive emotive behaviors on outwards occurrences instead of interpreting for themselves the representations of these events. In this regard, the ABC model for REBT was proposed.

The Diagnostic Step (ABC Theory)

A – The activating event: an occurrence that happens within your environment.

B – Beliefs: the beliefs that you have constructed about the events or circumstances.

C – Consequence: the emotive response you develop concerning your beliefs.

This model illustrates that it is not the triggering event A that causes your response to a situation but rather your belief that you have developed about such events that affect your overall response.

Let us use a working example to see what the illustrations engrained in the model:

A – Your spouse has filed for a divorce.

B – You believe he or she is doing this because you are not financially well off.

C – You feel low about your financial position.

Using the same illustration, if you had a different belief, your response will be quite different from the events. Let us look at this using the same premise but with a different opinion.

A - Your spouse has filed for a divorce.

B – You believe he or she is doing this because you have not been there when they need you the most.

C – You feel disappointed for letting your spouse down.

Looking at the illustrations, you can see that the same event has two different emotional responses that are holistically based on the belief that you have constructed about the event. As a result, the ABC model suggests that it is not the circumstances (A) that stimulate an emotional response but rather, the belief (B) that you have about the event that affects your reaction (C).

Main Beliefs of Rational Emotive Behavior

The Three Basics of Irrational Thinking

There is a variation of three common beliefs that are regarded as musts that formulate irrational thoughts that are founded on the demands of others, the environment, and ourselves. These three musts of irrational thought processes are:

1. I should accomplish great success to win the approval of others, and if that's not the case, then I am not good

2. Other people should handle me compassionately and fairly, and also in the same way that I want them to treat me. If I am not dealt with this way, they are bad people that need to be punished.

3. I should always have what I want when I want it, and how I want it. In this case, I must never get

what I don't want. If I don't have what I want, then I am dejected.

If you are not accorded "Must 1", you are more likely to feel depressed and anxious and even some instances guilty and shameful. In regards to "Must 2", when you are not handled relative to your perception, you may feel angry and act violently towards others. Finally, the failure to get "Must 3" leaves you having self-pity that may lead you into deferment.

Challenging Irrational Beliefs and Changing Your Emotional Response

The next phase of the REBT healing process is challenging the irrational beliefs that we believe we are encountering. In this framework, what you are analyzing are the developed unfounded assumptions such as questioning your philosophies; who says that if I do not win someone's endorsement, I am not good anymore? Once you can challenge your illogical thoughts, then you are now ready to replace these attitudes with healthier feelings and thoughts. This process is termed as the productive philosophy to a new life in which you challenge the three "Musts" and question their validity, while successively embracing practical ideas. In this framework, you will start your arguing within these terms:

"Instead of feeling low about my financial position that my spouse is feeling for a divorce, I will feel annoyed and get determined to solve things both on my end and on his or her end."

The three significant insights into REBT that you should familiarize yourself with in terms of depression and anxiety is that:

1. People should understand that the primary sources of their stress are the belief that they have developed about an event or circumstance.

2. When you acquire irrational beliefs, you should challenge them failure to which, you will hold on to these ideas, and it is those ideas that will continue upsetting you in your current state or the future.

3. These insights do not make us better, but it encourages us to develop more rational thoughts that are healthier to our wellbeing, and it should be cultured into you through the continuous practice of replacing irrational thoughts with positive ones.

The goal of Rational Emotive Behavior Therapy

The purpose of REBT is instilled inside its domain and course of the healing process that enables you to alter your beliefs about an event and channel new feelings into your thinking. As a result, REBT aims to replace your current philosophies with new ideas that promote positive healing and is flexible since it seeks to bring you happiness.

Hence, negative thoughts can be evaded by filling your belief process with realistic and rational beliefs. As earlier on stated, your understanding of an event is what causes the emotional response you demonstrate about the event, and your emotional reaction affects your behavior. This overlap of belief, emotional response, and practice once again boil down to the action changing your feelings about events, since you want to rationalize how you behave with your beliefs. Hence, it is a cycle that should be broken for you to be free from bleak or restless spirits by having the same period embrace positive thoughts.

This formulates the basis of REBT, to help you rational your beliefs and embrace positive philosophies. REBT achieves this goal by giving a diagnostic process in which you question the validity of your opinion, after which you analyze the consequences of such beliefs and how they are affecting you. It will come out surprising that the dogmas that are holding you back fall in the three "Musts" are not rational. In this case, having realistic thoughts about an event is what is encouraged through REBT.

The Models of Rational Emotive Behavior Therapy

The models of REBT are based on the major ABC archetypal that questions your irrational beliefs and gives you a new positive light on the circumstances surrounding the event. Some of the models involved in REBT are techniques such as; problem-solving techniques, cognitive restructuring, and coping.

Problem-Solving Model

The strategies involved in this model are founded on addressing the activating event (A) and consists of acquiring skills such as assertiveness, social skills, and decision-making skills. Examining these skills, then you are bound to realize that they help propel you into challenging the beliefs that you have based on the ideal ABC archetype. Then use these skills to successively construct positive mindsets that will help you through your healing process.

Cognitive Restructuring

This mode of REBT helps you to manage the unrealistic philosophy you hold in (B). Cognitive restructuring models involve the use of techniques such as;

1. Logical techniques that encourage you to have a more rational thinking capability without limiting yourself in one constrained irrational thoughts that affect your level of wellbeing.

2. Guided imagery and visualization technique will guide you into realizing the disadvantageous position that your beliefs place you and similarly get a clear image of how replacing these negative thoughts with better serving beliefs.

3. Reframing and looking at events differently, involves both logical and guided imagery techniques. The integration of these two techniques results in reframing your events. In this regard, you look at the occurrences in a different light.

Coping

Under coping, you are enhanced with clear visibility of managing (C) of irrational thoughts. Some of the techniques used under this model include:

1. Relaxation

2. Hypnosis.

3. Meditation.

These three techniques are geared towards helping you attain a stable mental state, which is peaceful and calm, and subsequently, help you realize your inner happiness.

Gain Insight and Recognize Irrational Thought Patterns

Although REBT helps you develop rational thoughts, it does not enable you to gain insights and recognize irrational thought patterns. Cognitive-behavioral therapy (CBT) comes out as an approach that you can use to identify some of the irrational thought patterns that you may develop. Through CBT, you can locate an absurd thought that is creating an emotive response, and once you have identified these thoughts, then you limit their power to take control over you. And the longer, irrational thought patterns are allowed to persist, the more they are engrained in your thinking and become part of your newly conceived reality.

Some of the irrational thought patterns include:

Catastrophizing involves having a biased and detrimental outcome of an event or about everything. This illogical thought pattern is mainly found in people with an anxiety disorder. In some instances, the fact that you view that going out and mingling with people will evoke the unsocial side of you, and people will be disgusted with you, probably hate, you, and you will be left with no friends. Having this thought pattern is irrational since you have a preconceived notion about an event in a negative light and not the constructivism required.

Minimization entails diminishing your good qualities while subsequently failing to see the good or bad conditions of others. This thought process is irrational since you have skewed thinking in which you fail to look at the concept in a different light.

Personalization is a particular form of splendor in which you believe you are the center of the universe, and everything revolves around you. This is a type of irrational thought pattern that encourages to have the belief that everything happening in one way or the other revolves around the actions that you showcase. For instance, a football fan may feel that the reason his or her team wins is that they put on their lucky clothes.

Failure to don in such an outfit, they have the perception that their team will lose. Having such a belief is unfounded since you cannot determine the outcomes of events that you are not directly involved in.

Magical Thinking, on the other end, is most common among children and adults who are suffering from obsessive-compulsive disorder. People who have bipolar disorders also experience this type of irrational thought pattern. Magical thinkers have the conception that certain rituals that they perform can protect them from impending danger or harm to themselves or others. In many instances, the undertaken routine is not reflective of the perceived risk and is continuously kept secret. With this kind of thought process, magical thinkers think that the habits that they perform will bring out a positive outcome, something which is not valid.

Grandiosity is a destructive thought pattern in which you hold an exaggerated sense of self-importance. With this thought pattern, you are disposed of at viewing yourself highly regarding specific events. For example, someone may feel they are the best at telling jokes and hold this perception, including wanting people to acknowledge they are the best even when they have a contrary opinion. When you continuously demonstrate this thought pattern, you become irrational since you have a more subjective opinion about yourself rather than an objective viewpoint.

Delusional Thinking stems out as the most irrational thought pattern of the discussed trends above. This is because it makes you hold delusional beliefs that are far from reality and have no objective truth in them.

Leaps in logic entail making accounts whose foundation missed some crucial steps. An example is jumping into conclusion, often negative ones with examining the information at hand to guide you into the process of making founded decisions. One instance of leaps in logic is the assumption that everyone will naturally know what you are thinking; this causes misunderstandings when someone cannot comprehend the ideas that you are trying to put across because you have engaged in an irrational thought process.

Chapter 7 Identify Negative Thoughts Patterns

Nearly everybody has experienced two kinds of thoughts. These forms of thoughts are one that offers encouragement and also critics an individual. These forms of thought are always with people nearly on a day to day basis. They have the potential to affect the day an individual has since they shape our perception of things and experiences life offers. The focus is vehemently drawn to the negative form of thoughts that is also known as the gremlin. The effect this form of thinking has on an individual is detrimental. Especially when these forms of thoughts keep on a recurring day in day out.

There are several steps that an individual can use to identify such thoughts. The steps are divided into two parts.

Part One

Identification of the running commentary running in one's head

The best depiction can be used by a movie. Certain movies have audio commentary tracks that run in them. There are situations that an individual is immersed in watching what the director and the actors are saying, there are other moments when an individual focuses only on what is happening on the screens. The inner thoughts in an individual brain at times behave the same way. Several thoughts crisscross the mind even if an individual does not pay attention. These thoughts have a very important influence on how an individual perceives several things. Therefore, it is very critical for an individual to pause and just have a take at the commentary in his or her brain.

Accept the thoughts if they are negative

The inner thoughts of a normal human being cannot be supportive and positive all the time. Various people who experience anxiety attacks are prone to experiencing this form of negative thoughts. A good example is an individual who is about to cliff to cliff dive and motivates him or herself to do the activity despite not knowing to swim. However, these thoughts are discouraged when an individual is about to do an easy test and he or she thinks he or she won't pass.

Using individual feeling as the cue for examining one's thoughts

There are several moments that people cannot have themselves attuned to our thoughts. People can be listeners to their thoughts for a long time and get nothing done. However, there are several emotional signs that negative thoughts can seem to portray. These feelings are very important when portrayed and need examination. These moments are associated with an individual being anxious or worried. Once these emotions are portrayed, an individual can start the process of examining his or her thoughts. Through paying close attention, he or she can eventually pursue the right course of action.

Part Two

Figuring out if one is filtering

The negative form of thinking can be derived from several forms of topics in the current globe. It is predicted to be derived from a familiar set of general forms. One of these forms is described as filtering. The form of filtering comes into play when an individual secludes positive thoughts from negative thoughts in certain situations. After secluding these thoughts, an individual then picks to handle things with negative thoughts. An elucidation can be used by an individual who has won the lottery. The ideology of filtering comes in to play when this individual only thinks about taxes, the fee to be paid to financial advisors and hand out to be given to friends.

Perceive if one is personalizing

There are several instances when a person can blame him or herself. An individual can blame himself, for example, blaming the rain because he or she wanted to go out. A person can also take it out on sports saying a certain team always loses when he or she watches. The two depictions are the best elucidation of what we talk about as personalizing things. It is a bad form of handling unwanted emotions when an individual blames him or herself. A person can also blame him or herself in an instance when his or her parents' divorce. The common form of thought is crossing an individual's mind is maybe he or she is the reason they were not happy.

Catching oneself catastrophizing

This moment entails a person anticipating the worst of things to happen in life. Such thoughts include an individual predicting that it may rain during the wedding day; he can anticipate that he or she won't be able to park the vehicle accurately or he or she will die alone. It is not bad when an individual is preparing for the worst things to happen. But is a bad case when an individual is experiencing these thoughts amid of contrary evidence. This is a depiction of having negative thoughts.

Picking up the habit of polarizing

Several people have a different perception of themselves and the world surrounding them. The perception is normally in a rigid binary fashion. The binary fashion includes seeing things either good or bad, white or black and yes or no. People who exemplify this form of thought tend to complicate various things because they don't have middle grounds. People who have the thought of polarizing effect only seething as either failure or success.

Judging if one is jumping into conclusions

This is a form of negative thinking and is similar to drawing assumptions on the negative side. The occurrence entails having the worst case of thoughts to an event even before their outcome is released. These situations do not provide any reason for an individual to having such thoughts. People tend to predict the worst case if they made a mistake during an interview. However, an individual should remain patient until the outcome is witnessed.

Observing if one is self-limiting

An individual can limit his or her chances of succeeding by creating a self-fluffing prophecy. The process of self-fulfilling prophecy was angering when an individual already makes up his or her mind before the completion of anything. The thought of self-limiting comes in to play from negative thoughts that limit someone's potential artificially. This poses a bigger threat to a person's achievements and happiness.

Homing in one's habits of speech

Several bad habits are created by negative thinking by an individual. People might not realize what they say at the moment but it comes to be detrimental in the future. A good depiction occurs when an individual calls him or herself stupid after committing a mistake. If this action is done several times, it has to push someone's image internally with time. It is because it develops as a normal assumption with time.

Observing how one makes other people's thoughts his or her own

When an individual is always blamed about every mistake he or she does, or during corrections is told he or she owed to do certain things; it proves to be a worse case in the future. This is despite an individual holding on to the advice. It is because the words and thoughts from the external environment affect a person. They make an individual have negative thoughts of guilt.

Chapter 8 Find negative thoughts in regular day to day existence

Fears, doubts, put-downs, presumptions of disappointment. You name the negative idea and I am almost certain I thought it at any rate once in my lifetime. It would be more than safe to state I have been known to be a glass half void sort of young lady. Yet, you know what I have figured it out? These negative contemplations hinder each enormous objective I have for myself. Keeping me away from finding the affection for my life, from seeking after a vocation I am genuinely energetic about, from having truly compensating kinships with others, from taking risks throughout everyday life and getting a charge out existing apart from everything else thus significantly more.

Whenever you need to change your conditions, you have to change the manner in which you think. You need to quit accepting that you are stuck in your site never-seriously tolerating that you're unequipped for taking care of business. Numerous individuals enable themselves to be confined by their dread and uneasiness. For these individuals, an inward pundit consistently is by all accounts murmuring in their ears, shielding them from succeeding. Truly, negative reasoning. They will shackle you to a life that is both fair and unfulfilling. In the event that you need to extend yourself to your fullest potential, you have to get away from your deliberate jail of negative reasoning.

Eventually, your musings are maybe the most significant piece of any new objective you set for yourself and in the event that they are fundamentally in the negative classification how would you think your objectives are going to play out. Yea, they will most likely get added to the ceaseless "objectives incomplete" show you as of now have. Perhaps, you imagine a scenario in which you took a stab at something other than what's expected. Envisage a scenario in which you could deal with calming those negative musings and opening up space in your cerebrum. Far better, imagine a scenario in which you could supplant them with positive musings. What an idea right?!

Here is my bit by bit plan for halting negative reasoning (I urge you to try it out!):

Make a decision.

It may sound self-evident; however, you don't understand how regularly we are half in and half out with our objectives. We state we need something, however despite everything we question it will occur or HOW it will occur?

Tune in, you can't make sense of how to get something going in the event that you don't initially choose you are all in. So, settle on a decision about what you need for your year.

Do you pick joy? Victory? Love? Trust? Confidence?

Whatever it is you have to clear on this decision since when negative contemplations creep back in you should begin back now.

Get very close to your negative contemplations.

It's hard to believe, but it's true, we rush to bounce to the positive reasoning and demands we are mystically not going to think about. I prefer not to break it to you; however, your psyche doesn't work that way.

Opposing your negative considerations is simply going to make them that a lot more grounded. You would prefer not to sustain that bear. So, all things being equal you really need to recognize those negative contemplations.

Highlight the considerable number of fears, questions, negative contemplations you have about yourself in your mind. I need you to get past legit with yourself here, possibly recording a few things that are truly mean.

You must get them out of your cerebrum so as to make space for other progressively positive considerations to come in.

Sympathetically tell your negative musings you needn't bother with them.

So, you've recorded each one of those mean and negative musings and now you can nicely tell them they are not required. Recognize your feelings of trepidation for attempting to ensure you, yet in addition let yourself realize that you decide not to require those defensive negative considerations today.

You are going to take a stab at something else. These means may be rehashed again and again as circumstances spring up that test your inspiration aptitudes.

Get back to reality.

Negative reasoning is frequently based on thinking about the past that is upsetting, harmful or frustrating, or around nervousness or misgiving about something that we accept will occur later on. These agonizing or dreadful considerations keep us from concentrating on the present and tolerating where we are right now in time.

Negative thinking makes tension and mental torment since we are centered around these ruminations as opposed to living in the truth existing apart from everything else. By taking your consideration back to the present, you'll see that your negative contemplations are only that - musings. They aren't real. By living at the time, you can start to shape your existence the manner in which you need.

Become an agreeable individual.

If you intend to break free of antagonism, you're going to need to begin pulling in the positive. That implies oozing the sort of constructive vitality that makes individuals need to incline toward you. This can be possible by figuring out how to be straightforward, active and affable. Do you make individuals feel good around you? Do you show enthusiasm for them and get some information about themselves (and afterward truly tune in to their answers)?

We as a whole need to feel acknowledged and loved, and in the event that you demonstrate this thought to other people, they will start to react in kind. You can begin by moving the concentration from yourself to others by demonstrating people around you that you genuinely care for them. Become an "agreeable individual" by first getting to be OK with yourself and making others feel welcome and acknowledged when they are around you.

The intensity of change lies within.

To break the negative cycle, you have turned out to be caught in, you should acknowledge that the ability to change - to grasp the positive - must originate from inside. Nobody else can do this for you. You should be equipped for reframing your attitude by grasping and making positive changes.

The initial step is to start moving endlessly from being totally self-engaged, self-retained and enveloped by a skeptical outlook. Start concentrating on approaches to indicate empathy and comprehension toward others.

Recognize something you feel needs improvement; something that will help other people. Engage in an association or a reason that is greater than yourself, and feel that it is so elating to concentrate on making something positive as opposed to being caught by the negative. Perceive that at last you should be the one to make a more beneficial, increasingly positive you.

Understanding emotions with the technique for CBT

In CBT, emotion remains with idea and conduct as one of the cooperating components that make up an individual's internal life. In this methodology, every one of the three is viewed as associated and affecting each other: Emotion may flag the nearness of significant restorative material in the psychological or conduct domain, and likewise, practices and contemplations could add to creating unhelpful feelings, for example, ceaseless nervousness.

The acknowledgment that every irregular bystander is carrying on with a real existence as clear and mind-boggling as your own – populated with their very own aspirations, companions, schedules, stresses and acquired madness – an epic story that proceeds undetectably around you like an ant colony dwelling place rambling profound underground, with expound ways to a huge number of different lives that you'll never know existed, in which you may show up just once, as an extra tasting espresso out of sight, as a haze of traffic passing on the roadway, like a lit window at nightfall.

Have you at any point simply set aside the effort to watch the individuals around you? In case you have, at that point you will have mulled over the way that everybody has a rich internal enthusiastic world. Everybody is at the focal point of their own story, with their own legends and miscreants, plot turns, battles and victories. We as a whole need to live glad lives, so for what reason do we discover it so hard some of the time?

One well-known hypothesis in brain research is that individuals are not developed to be upbeat, yet rather are 'intended' for endurance. In the event that that is valid, at that point it changes the standards of the game apiece. Our activity winds up one of understanding how we can occupy these brains and bodies that are intended for endurance rather than joy, and to live the best lives that we can. In this section we will realize why feelings are significant, and consider a portion of the manners in which they can meddle with our lives.

The motivation behind emotions

Q: Why do we have emotions?

A: Emotions spur us, they make us need to get things done.

How about we do a speedy psychological study. Envision you woke up one day and didn't have any feelings. How might you choose what to do that day? How might you know what's significant and so forth? Perhaps you didn't have any feelings would it feel 'pleasant' to be in a warm, agreeable bed? OK feel amped up for getting down to business? Or then again stressed over what might occur in the event that you turned out poorly? Imagine a scenario where you had figured out how to get up and were going across the street – would you try to hustle if a vehicle was coming towards you. Why try to do anything by any means?

Our feelings help to manage the choices that we make each moment of our lives. Our general surroundings (and the contemplations in our minds) trigger passionate responses constantly. Quite a bit of what we do is inspired by a longing to change or keep up an inclination state – to clutch nice sentiments or to maintain a strategic distance from awful emotions.

Various emotions inspire us to act in various manners

Have you at any point had the inclination to yell at somebody who was angering you? Or on the other hand the desire to give somebody an embrace when they were extremely pitiful? Do you ever truly needed to take the last bit of cake? These desires are driven by our feelings. Feelings make us need to act, and various feelings control us towards various types of activities. We don't need to act in the manner our feelings propose, yet everybody has had the experience of needing to accomplish something.

Assume Responsibility for Your Emotions with CBT

We frequently accept we are helpless before circumstances and occasions. The long queue at the bank made us upset. What that individual said got us discouraged. There are such a large number of circumstances in our lives that have the ability to make us feel cheerful or pitiful, irate or quiet.

But then, is that truly what's going on? Does the circumstance really control our temperaments and feelings?

In the field of CBT there is a typical schoolwork task. In this task, you take a sheet of note pad paper, make three vertical sections and recognize the left one as A, the center one as B and the correct one as C.

Segment A	Segment B	Segment C

The A-segment is for the Antecedent. This is the circumstance or the occasion that makes us feel the manner in which we do. Segment C is for the mind-set or feeling, expedited from that circumstance in segment A

Segment A	Segment B	Segment C
Situation		Mood/Emotion

We regularly trust A causes C. The circumstance causes the disposition or feeling. Be that as it may, there is this center section, B. This section is our conviction about the circumstance. Our conviction is the thing that interprets, channels and offers importance to the circumstance that offers ascend to our temperaments and feelings, just as choices and practices. It is this B section that CBT investigates and looks at – and gives apparatuses by which the conviction can be changed. At the point when the conviction about the circumstance is changed, the state of mind or feeling we experience is additionally changed. And after that our choices change. We act in an unexpected way.

Segment A	Segment B	Segment C
Situation		Mood/Behavior

As a functional model, how about we take a gander at a normal circumstance, for example, the road turned parking lot. You're in a road turned parking lot, and you are ending up progressively irritated. In a customary CBT style, we would record in the A section, "congested driving conditions." In the C segment, we record our mind-set or feeling, for example, furious. (Note: we do this activity afterward, not while we are in the vehicle driving!)

Segment A	Segment B	Segment C
Traffic jam		Angry

In the B section we record our conviction about the circumstance; maybe we think being in a road turned parking lot isn't reasonable, it isn't right, it ought not occur, it's the deficiency of the city organizers, it will make you late to work, and on the off chance that you are late to work, your activity is in danger, which at that point implies you will be seen as flighty, and on the off chance that you are unreliable, at that point you are powerless, and amateurish, and possibly useless.

Segment A	Segment B	Segment C
Traffic jam	Unfair	Angry

Be that as it may, convictions are not actualities. They are progressively similar to conclusions — they are regularly subjective, there is frequently no proof to help them, they can even be incorrect to the point of being misrepresentations, lies. Our convictions — mistaken, discretionary or accurate — are genuinely settled and offer significance to the circumstance. In light of that importance, we have a state of mind or a feeling from which we settle on choices and act on them. Given the power our convictions have on our states of mind, feelings, choices and practices, is it not advantageous to address them?

Taking a gander at our convictions is a significant advance towards emotional well-being. Our convictions about circumstances can have a significant effect. It is here, in working with Segment B, where a prepared CBT is useful.

Working with a CBT specialist can help you in finding the incorrect or useless convictions and work with you to move them towards an increasingly balanced and useful perspective on a circumstance, yourself and your reality.

From that we become engaged. Our circumstances never again control our dispositions, feelings, choices and practices. We are more in direction. We could even get ourselves less irate, maybe quiet during a congested road, also the different testing employment-related and relationship circumstances in which we wind up connected day by day.

Automatic Negative Thoughts (ANTs)

Automatic Negative Thoughts (ANTs) are musings that are automatically actuated in specific circumstances. In misery, ANTs normally focus on subjects of pessimism, low confidence, and futility. For instance, when confronting an undertaking, ANTs might be 'I will come up short'. In nervousness issues, programmed musings frequently incorporate overestimations of hazard and underestimations of capacity to adapt. Numbers bandied about from numerous sources demonstrate that grown-ups have somewhere close to 60,000 to 80,000 musings every day. Most are tedious and many are negative. Two significant inquiries call to be replied:

- Where do the contemplations begin?

- What would we say we are to do with them?

The reaction to the main originates from a segment of the cerebrum known as the claustrum. It is characterized as, "a slight, sporadic, sheet-like neuronal structure covered up underneath the inward surface of the neocortex." It is associated with the turning on of considerations.

The reaction to the second is similarly confounded. As I am composing this piece, my psyche is inundated with various musings that force my consideration from the main job. All through some random day, my psychological meanderings take me based on what is before me to interruptions, for example, thinking about how I will deal with pending difficulties, to what issues my patient will bring to our sessions, from innovative thoughts enticing me to follow up on them to the topic of whether I need to go to the rec center to work it out or return to rest. A few days it appears as though I am crowding little cats who are resolved to escape the house. I credit it to the maturing procedure by which the musings spill through the openings in my strainer like cerebrum. I state that the hard drive gets full and that the issue isn't capacity, however recovery. I am chuckling as I understand that my brain is especially similar to the PC on which I am composing with various tabs open as I explore.

In Buddhist practice, it is alluded to as the monkey mind that prattles and jumps from tree to tree, similar to its tendency and is considered, "agitated, fretful, impulsive, eccentric; whimsical, capricious, confounded; hesitant, wild". I compare it to the youngsters' down called Barrel of Monkeys. That plastic compartment in essential hues loaded up with little simians with bent tails and arms move players to get whatever a number of them in a chain as could be expected under the circumstances without dropping them. The disappointment is that occasionally more than one monkey hops on board when endeavoring to get together each in turn. Usually, a route with our contemplations. What number is clamoring for our consideration and how would we appropriately address them without being immersed?

The vast majority claim they have swarms of ANTs to manage. Uneasiness is an ongoing theme for them that range from stresses over wellbeing to endeavoring to explore the relationship waters, from worries in the working environment to deciding how to traverse every day with some similarity to unblemished mental soundness. We work our way through them using testing the legitimacy of their contemplations. Frequently, they reprimand themselves for what they can't control and once in a while divert duty regarding what they may have done another way. Consolidating CBT, they are getting to be skilled at driving the ANTs out of the entryway.

We likewise use a four-advance procedure that is a significant compact apparatus to offer an option.

- Facts – what truly occurred?

- Perception-how they see it.

- Judgment-what they make it mean.

- Action to determine them-steps to roll out an improvement.

Frequently the musings will break up and the ANTS disperse when these means are applied.

An example:

Somebody accepts that they will never prevail in their field of undertaking since they haven't by the normal point in their life. They went after a position for which they weren't contracted. The common idea was that they were sick prepared or generally not deserving of the position. Certainly is, they didn't land the position. Observation is, "I am imperfect and clumsy." Judgment is, "I will never be sufficient for this or any activity that I need." The activity step is to re-compose the account, modify their methodology that may incorporate making a rundown of their positive credits and ranges of abilities to bring to the table, and be increasingly arranged for the following chance.

Telling the truth while tidying up the ANTS in my mind:

When I am complimented on my abilities, I now and then default to, "Yeh, right... on the off chance that I'm all that and a pack of chips, at that point why I'm not increasingly fruitful by common gauges and coming in the mixture?"

As I set out on new pursuits, I have would in general uncertainty that I will execute them faultlessly. (Who revealed to me that anything must be faultless?)

Investigating my shoulder to note if the 'legitimacy police' are watching to check whether I am in fact 'doing it right'.

Stress over overlooking significant data.

Watching for the unavoidable conclusion.

Envisioning dissatisfaction.

Falling prey to 'insufficient it - is' and sham disorder.

Tools to bring the monkey-psyche to quietude and shoo the ANTs away:

- Breathing with a plume before your nose. Envision you are breathing in your preferred aroma and inhale out gradually as though smothering birthday candles.

- Place one hand on your brow and the other on the occipital edge behind your head as though giving it a delicate embrace. Breathe in through your nose and breathe out through your mouth and murmur.

- Lay one hand on your stomach and the other in your heart and breathe in through your nose and out through your mouth as you envision associating the two body parts.

- Hold two hands open before you, palms up as though you are measuring water. At that point take each thumb and individually address each finger gradually as you state to yourself, "I am quiet.", "I am loose.", "I am quiet at this point." and, "Everything is great at this point."

Non-functional assumptions

These are conditional convictions that shape one's reaction to encounters and circumstances. For instance, "Whenever that somebody draws near to me, they will find the 'genuine me' and reject me." These may work outside of the person's mindfulness and may not be unmistakably verbalized or the individual might know about these suspicions.

Interpersonal Strategies – Non-functional assumptions that emphasize explicitly on methods for affecting others. For instance, "The best approach to persuade kids to be great is the impact that the conviction has in the person's life (for example is it utilitarian or broken), not whether the conviction is sound or not. For instance, numerous individuals see the relational procedure "On the off chance that I need somebody to like me, I ought to be decent to them" as discerning. Be that as it may, this methodology can demonstrate to be broken except if it is matched with convictions that help fitting affirmation and breaking point setting.

Core beliefs

Core beliefs, or schemas, are profoundly held convictions about self, others, and the world. The core belief is, for the most part, adapted from the get-go throughout everyday life and are impacted by youth encounters and seen as outright. Core Beliefs – Unconditional beliefs that fill in as a reason for screening, sorting, and translating encounters. For instance, "I'm nothing more than a bad memory." "Others can't be believed." "Exertion doesn't satisfy." These frequently work outside of the person's mindfulness and regularly are not unmistakably verbalized.

You may see that the rundown above does exclude "diagram." There is an issue with the way "mapping" is utilized in CBT. Frequently the expression "diagram" is utilized just as it is synonymous with "center conviction". Be that as it may, "schema" had set up importance in brain research sometime before it wound up famous in intellectual conduct circles. Schemas can help in understanding the world. Most circumstances don't require effortful idea when utilizing pattern since programmed thought is all that is required. Individuals can compose new discernments into blueprints rapidly." Note that "schema" isn't equivalent to "core belief."

A schema is a steady system of core belief ("I'm nothing more than trouble"), contingent convictions ("If individuals draw near to me they'll find the "genuine me" and reject me"), relational methodologies ("I'll put on a beguiling façade and conceal every one of my deficiencies and weaknesses"), just as more subtle presumptions (Someone who cherishes me will realize what I need and do it without my asking them" and "If he's annoyed with me, he's dismissing me"). A center conviction is only one part of mapping. Likewise, note that the center conviction isn't the main part of an outline that can be broken. At different focuses through the span of CBT with a specific client, we may work to alter core beliefs, restrictive convictions, relational methodologies, as well as different convictions and suppositions. These are generally parts of blueprint change.

Shockingly, when "schema" is treated as if it implies a similar thing as "core belief", this is pointlessly befuddling. If CBT reliably utilized "center conviction" to allude to explicit core belief and utilized "schema" to allude to a moderately steady system of core belief, restrictive suppositions, relational methodologies, and related comprehensions, it would be simpler for us to impart obviously about this unpredictable point. Up to that point, when perusing or discussing "schemas" it will be imperative to focus on whether the other party truly implies schema, belief, or something different.

Chapter 9 Break Away From Negative Thoughts Patterns

We all struggle with automatic thoughts. These well examined in the practice of cognitive-behavioral therapy, in which it is taught that these are ideas, beliefs, or images that occur in response to a specific action, event, or another trigger. As their name implies, automatic thoughts pop into our minds without conscious effort or thought.

Automatic thoughts are not either good or bad, as they can be both. For instance, you might have an automatic thought telling you to "be careful" when you are walking alone to your car at night and hear something in the distance. Or, it might tell you to stop and double-check both sides of the road before crossing the street. But, these automatic thoughts when paired with cognitive distortions can lead to many negative thoughts and feelings. For instance, you may have automatic thoughts such as "I can't do this" when taking on a new challenge, or "everybody must hate me" when trying to talk to someone. These negative automatic thoughts must be challenged; otherwise, they will lead to a vicious cycle, worsen cognitive distortions, increase anxiety, and possibly even lead to depression.

With cognitive-behavioral therapy, you can learn to overturn your negative automatic thoughts and distortions with healthy and balanced thinking. You can learn to analyze your thoughts, finding which are true and false, which are helpful and unhelpful, and then use that knowledge to balance out your thinking. With practice, you will learn to negate negative thoughts and replace them with healthy thoughts until it becomes second nature.

As you learn to overcome your negative thought patterns, you will be able to live a happier and healthier life. You will learn to better care for yourself, those around you, and can better take on the challenges life throws at you. Over time, you will find coping with stress, anxiety, insomnia, depression, and intrusive thoughts easier and they may even greatly decrease.

Cognitive-behavioral therapy will teach you the techniques and practices you need, and by using these tools consistently, you will soon find that this healthier thinking comes more naturally. For instance, instead of thinking that everyone in the room must dislike you, you can accept that there will be both people who like and dislike you and that you can choose to talk to them in the hopes of making a good impression. Another example is if you got a bad grade on a paper you could accept that you didn't do your best and tell yourself that you can work towards improving rather than degrade yourself and assume you must be a failure.

With cognitive behavioral therapy, you can learn to overturn negative and distorted thinking, teaching yourself to stay on guard against negativity. Questions such as "Can I try better in the future?", "What exactly did the person say?", "Has anyone done anything to lead me to believe they dislike me?", and "What is a more balanced perspective" can help you to adjust your thinking and turn the negative into a positive.

It's important to learn that the harsh and negative views we hold of ourselves and life aren't always the truth. Use questions and affirmations to help yourself notice the positive and balance out the negative, in turn overcoming your distortions. For instance, you might use affirmations to remind yourself of the positive, such as "I worked hard this past week and I did my best, and the result of my hard work is that I learned and made a good impression on those around me. I will learn from my mistakes and improve further in the future. I can enjoy my successes while also learning from my mistakes."

Cognitive-behavioral uses many methods to help people overturn their negative thoughts and change how they think. A few of these methods include:

- Learning to notice negative or irrational thoughts

- Stopping these thoughts in their place

- Replacing negative and irrational thoughts with positive and more balanced thoughts

- How to relax both your mind and body to decrease stress

And, this is only the tip of the iceberg. Along with these methods, you can learn to incorporate positive affirmations into your daily routine. While many people have heard of the power of positive affirmations and self-talk, they have little understanding of the science behind this method and how to harness it for their benefit. They may try saying something positive to themselves in the mirror and not notice an improvement, and therefore think it isn't for them. But, this is largely due to people being unaware of how to use positive affirmations for their benefit and an unwillingness to stick with it.

If you practice using positive affirmations regularly, you will find that it can have an enormous and beneficial effect on your life and mental health. With practice, you will begin to handle stress better, view yourself in a better light, and even perceive the world as a whole differently.

To attain benefits from positive affirmations, you must learn at a fundamental level what they are and what they are not. When you struggle with negative and damaging thoughts or beliefs and cognitive distortions you can replace them with positive affirmations. These affirmations are perceived truths that we confidently tell ourselves and remind ourselves of to replace the negative distortions that we are prone to struggle with.

The goal of these affirmations isn't to puff up our chests or make us believe we are superior to other people or better than we are. Instead, the goal is to foster confidence, positivity, and unwind negative lies we believe. By repeating these affirmations regularly, you will be able to accept them as truth and are then less likely to believe the negative distortions you are prone to believe.

With regular practice, these affirmations can profoundly affect a person's self-confidence, optimism, positivity, and even the success they achieve. After all, a confident person is more likely to attain the success they seek than someone who is afraid and doesn't believe in themselves.

But, it is important to remember that affirmations on their own are not a solution to all of your problems. Instead, they are a piece of the puzzle of cognitive-behavioural therapy. To attain the benefits of CBT, you need to employ all of the methods found within this book, and not just one or two practices.

As there are many misconceptions about positive affirmations and self-talk, let's go over a couple of these misconceptions before going into detail on how you can practice these affirmations.

The goal of these positive affirmations is not to create a blind optimism, but rather the rewrite negative thoughts, break cognitive distortions, and promote positive thinking. The affirmations needed for these benefits will vary from person to person, as many of our negative thought processes and cognitive distortions were developed during our childhood and young adult lives. While what leads to these negative ideas may belong in the past, it can still affect us greatly and need to be confronted constructively.

This is why blind optimism and phrases such as "everything is perfect," or "I won't mess up," aren't constructive or helpful. Instead, phrases such as "I am prepared, but even if I make a mistake it will be okay, and I have the tools I need to handle it," and "I choose to find joy and see the good in life." While the first options promoted a false and unattainable idea of perfection, only setting a person up for disappointment, the second acknowledges that while life may not be perfect, we can choose how we react.

Positive affirmations are also not self-deception. The purpose of these phrases isn't to make you believe that your life is free of problems, that you don't mess up, that you don't have any responsibility, or that your stress if unfounded. Instead, the purpose is to help us acknowledge that while our stress may be understandable, we also have a habit of making our stress worse than it needs to be with negative thought patterns and distortions.

With an affirmation that is true and rooted in reality, you can learn to readjust your thought process and create firm and constructive intentions. As this is the true purpose of affirmations, it explains why people who try deceiving themselves with nice-sounding thoughts never experience the benefits that positive affirmations have to offer.

While it is best to use positive affirmations in conjunction with a complete cognitive behavioural therapy approach, one of the benefits of these affirmations is that you can benefit from the beginning immediately. Even before you finish reading this book, you can begin to implement positive affirmations and self-talk in your daily life to change your inner dialogue from something negative to something balanced. By beginning to implement positive affirmations immediately, you can get a head start on improved emotional and mental well-being, and prepare yourself to soon begin a CBT approach to your entire life for even more benefits.

To start practicing positive affirmations and self-talk begin with these simple and easy-to-follow steps:

Take Small Steps

When you begin the process of using positive affirmations and self-talk don't feel that you have to go from zero to one-hundred overnight. Instead, start with small steps to change your thoughts and inner dialogue. You can do this by taking note and analysing how you react to situations and words, and then ask yourself why it elicits the emotions you are experiencing.

Identify Your Negativity

When you notice that you have negative thoughts or emotions, then take a moment to stop and acknowledge that what you are feeling is negativity and identify what emotion you are feeling. Is the emotion fear? Guilt? Doubt? Anger? Shame? By acknowledging and identifying your thoughts and feelings, you can then deal with them.

Replace the Negative with Positive

After you have acknowledged and identified your negative thoughts, work towards replacing them with something more positive. For instance, rather than calling yourself an "idiot" replace it with something such as "I may have been ignorant on this matter, but I can learn and grow." If you are thinking "I'm a failure" you can replace it with "What matters is that I tried my best."

Balanced and True

When using positive affirmations and self-talk, it must be balanced and true if you want it to be effective and helpful. For instance, it wouldn't be helpful to tell yourself "I will never make a mistake," as you are only setting yourself up for failure and you very well know that you will make mistakes. On the other hand, if you tell yourself "I am prepared, and I will do my best" you are reminding yourself that even if you do make a mistake, you can handle it and it will be okay. This could be compared to creating business goals, which also have to be balanced and true. You wouldn't find it helpful to say "I'm going to make a million dollars the opening week of business," but it could be helpful to say "I will network with five people every day to grow my business."

Find Inspiration

When you are struggling with self-doubt, fear, anger, and other negative emotions it can be difficult to know what affirmations you need to help when beginning. Of course, over time it becomes easier, but at first, you are at a loss as you don't believe in yourself. But, there are many people you can reach out to for inspiration, you don't have to stand alone. Look for other people who use positive affirmations for inspiration; you don't even have to talk to them personally.

You can find a wide range of positive affirmations online that you can use or adapt to your situation.

Practice Regularly

If you hope to receive success and improvement from the use of positive affirmations and self-talk, you must practice on a regular day-to-day basis. After all, change doesn't happen overnight. You can't rewire your brain and thought process in a single day or even a week. Stick with using these positive affirmations, practicing using them daily for at least a month. I promise you if you follow all of these steps for a month you will notice a difference looking back. Practice using these positive affirmations when you wake up in the morning, before you go to sleep at night, and whenever you find yourself thinking negatively.

One of the wonderful aspects of positive affirmations and self-talk is that anyone can experience their benefits with a little knowledge, time, and practice. But, remember, if you hope to reap all of the benefits that positive affirmations have to offer, use them in conjunction with the other tools and practices written about in this book.

Along with using positive affirmations, you may also try to implement cognitive restructuring, which is one of the core principles of cognitive-behavioural therapy practice. Cognitive restructuring is similar to positive affirmations, and use some of the same steps, but it can be applied even more widely and have a greater benefit on cognitive distortions. To experience the most benefits, combine using both positive affirmations and cognitive restructuring.

Imagine that you write a report for school and get a pretty good grade. But, the teacher has some recommendations on how you can improve. While you may know that you did well, got a good grade, and they are only trying to help you improve, it may have hit a raw nerve. You feel upset, even though you know that you shouldn't. So, after you leave the situation you think it over, consider why you were upset and felt attacked, and then remind yourself that your teacher thought you did well and is only trying to help because they believe in you. After you take some time, you decide to take up your teacher's advice and apologize for taking out your frustrations in your conversation with them.

In this situation, you have used cognitive restructuring to overcome your negative thought process and emotions and change your thinking.
Cognitive restructuring is a helpful practice to overcome your automatic thoughts and emotions. With regular practice, you

will learn how to understand your thoughts and emotions so that you can then change them into something more balanced and healthy. You can learn to overcome untrue and unhelpful negative thoughts into something that will benefit both yourself and others. This is a practice that everyone can benefit from, as even people with few cognitive distortions will at times struggle with negative and untrue automatic thoughts. Along with benefiting peoples' relationships and stress levels, cognitive restructuring has also been used in the treatment of anxiety, depression, post-traumatic stress disorder, phobias, addictions, and more.

You will find that as you use cognitive restructuring your approach to situations changes and your mood improves. This allows you to have better interactions with others and increase your productivity. When struggling with negative moods and unpleasant thoughts it's simply more difficult to interact with others and be productive, but with cognitive restructuring, you can turn this around!

To utilize and benefit from cognitive restructuring try following these eight steps regularly:

Calm Your Mind

If you are struggling with emotions, then you may have trouble confronting the thoughts behind the emotions. Therefore, first, calm your mind by using deep breathing or meditation until your stress decreases and you can think more easily and calmly.

Identify the Trigger

After you have calmed down identify and describe the trigger that caused you to become upset, whether it was a specific situation or phrase.

Analyse Your Emotions

Calmly analyse your emotions and what you were feeling during the triggering circumstance. When describing your emotions and moods keep in mind that this is different from thoughts. Psychologists explain that while moods and emotions are often explainable in a single word or two, the thoughts behind these emotions are more complex and require complete sentences to explain. For instance, you may feel the emotions anger or humiliation, but your thoughts behind these emotions are that you are angry that your significant other made a joke at your expense in front of your friends and you now feel humiliated because of it.

Identify Your Automatic Thoughts

The automatic thoughts you are experiencing are the thoughts that you first experienced in the moment and as a reaction to your emotions. For instance, in the situation above your automatic thoughts may be:

"My significant other doesn't respect me."

"My friends think I'm weak."

"Everyone must think I'm a joke."

"I'm alone in this world."

All of these are automatic thoughts caused by the situation and emotions. But, the most disturbing or distressing thoughts are known as "hot thoughts." In this situation, the hot thoughts are *"everyone must think I'm a joke,"* and *"I'm alone in this world."*

Search for Supportive Evidence

After writing out a list of your emotions and automatic thoughts, search for objective evidence that supports these thoughts. For instance, you might write:

"My friends laughed along to the joke."

"My significant other repeatedly makes jokes at my expense."

The goal of this is to objectively look at the facts, and then write down specific circumstances that lead to your automatic thoughts.

Search for Contradictory Evidence

After searching for objective evidence that supports your automatic thoughts, you must search for objective evidence that contradicts these thoughts. In this case, this evidence might be:

"My friends seemed to have been awkwardly laughing."

"I've never seen my friends make jokes at my expense."

"My significant other is awkward when meeting people."

"I've never told my significant other that I don't like jokes at my expense."

"Both my friends and significant others are always supportive."

After looking at both lists, you can see that there is more evidence contradicting your fears and concern. It is fair to be hurt, but instead of lashing out in anger and embarrassment, it is better to talk over the issue with the people involved calmly.

Find Balanced and Fair Thoughts

By this step, you have calmed your mind and looked objectively at the situation. You should now have the ability to analyse the situation and create a more balanced and fair view of the triggering circumstance. If you are having a difficult time doing this on your own, then you may find help in discussing it with someone else and testing out your new ideas to see if they are balanced. When asking someone to listen, ensure that it is someone who is also balanced and fair rather than someone who gets angry or emotional easily. Just as you did with the previous steps, be sure to write down your new views and ideas as you think of them. By writing down each step, you will have an easier time focusing and will better be able to consider new ideas. Some new and balanced ideas of the above situation might include:

"What my significant other said hurt and embarrassed me, but I know that wasn't their intent."

"I trust my friends, their laughter hurt but I'm sure that they simply did not know how to respond, I will ask them about it calmly."

"Instead of getting angry, I will calmly ask my significant other to please refrain from making jokes at my expense. Open communication is important in every relationship."

"The joke wasn't anything negative, but it hit a raw nerve which is why it hurt. I'm sure nobody knew it caused me pain."

Analyse Your New Mood

After following the previous steps, you should be able to think much more clearly and have a better view of the situation. Reanalyse your mood and see if it has improved, and then write down the results of how you feel.

135

After you understand your new emotional state ask yourself what you can do to improve the situation. You may no longer need to take action, you may want to calmly discuss it with the other person(s) involved, or you may want to apologize if you found that you lashed out in anger.

Lastly, use positive affirmations to help yourself learn to better react to similar situations that may occur at some point in the future.

The use of positive affirmations and cognitive restructuring is greatly beneficial in replacing negative thoughts with something more balanced and positive. It will take time, but practice using these methods daily and before long you will find that your entire thought process changes and that your cognitive distortions become more balanced.

Chapter 10 Choose Alternatives That Are Neutral or Positive

Life is indeed complex. Some things are black and white. And then some other things have a gray area. Many people develop chronic anxiety as a result of their failure to recognize that success cannot be defined in definite terms. For instance, if market forces conspire to make your business fall off the race, must you label yourself a failure and develop anxiety? By no means! First off, there's no true meaning of success. In other words, success is what you want it to be for you might have unconventional metrics to measure it. Not everybody attaches financial milestones to success. Thus, failure to look at the gray areas of life can lead to needless development of anxieties. In the case above, acknowledging that even if you didn't make a ton of money with your business, you played a critical role in society by providing a product or service that had been greatly needed. Thinking in black-and-white terms only intensifies your emotional polarity and when things don't go as you expected you are not going to take drastic actions. CBT helps you glance at the areas that you neglect s you are consumed by your apparent loss or humiliation.

Alternatives to Cognitive Behavioral Therapy

Since the discovery of CBT and REBT, many other psychologists and doctors have gone on to study these forms of therapies and create their own alternatives to CBT, too. It appears that when Beck and Ellis discovered the power of the cognitive mind, everyone realized that this was the most effective way forward and decided to put it to the test. As a result, a few other forms of therapy were developed that follow a similar framework and lead to the healing of depression and other mood disorders, too.

The four most commonly recognized alternatives to CBT include REBT, Dialectical Behavioral Therapy (DBT), Exposure and Response Prevention Therapy (ERP), and Acceptance and Commitment Therapy (ACT).

Although this book is not going to teach you how to use these alternative therapies, we will discuss what they are and how they work. Recognizing that they work on a similar framework as CBT might help you recognize the power of CBT itself and the capacity it has to support you in healing from depression. As well, if you find that certain concepts in CBT do not make sense or do not seem to help you as much as you wish, you can always look into these alternatives and create a combination approach to support you in healing from your depression. At the end of the day, the most important thing is that you find what works for you and that you apply it consistently so that you can develop the necessary skills, strength, and resiliency to overcome your depression.

Dialectical Behavioral Therapy (DBT)

DBT is a form of therapy that supports patients in discovering new skills that they can use to help them manage their painful emotions. They can also use these skills to decrease conflict in their relationships so that they are more likely to experience healthier and happier relationships with themselves, their peers, their family and friends, and their romantic partners.

DBT focuses on four key areas where patients are encouraged to build and nurture skills within themselves. These key areas include mindfulness, distress tolerance, emotion regulation, and interpersonal effectiveness. With mindfulness, the individual is taught how they can become more capable of accepting their present reality and staying grounded in the present moment. With distress tolerance, individuals are taught how to increase their tolerance to stressful situations so that they are less likely to experience such massive stress responses. For emotional regulation, people are taught how to regulate their intense emotions so that their emotions are less likely to cause problems in their lives. When it comes to interpersonal effectiveness, patients are taught to communicate in a way with others that is assertive while also maintaining their self-respect and improving the quality of their relationships with others.

Exposure and Response Prevention Therapy (ERP)

Exposure and Response Prevention Therapy have one primary goal when it comes to supporting patients with overcoming their challenges in life. The goal is to support those who are having excessive obsessive thoughts refrain from actually engaging in those thoughts with compulsions or habitual behaviors. ERP focuses on exposing people to things gradually over time while also giving those skills on how to navigate the exposures effectively. This way, their maladaptive responses can be overcome, and they can begin to learn how to navigate their obsessions more intentionally, rather than being taken over by habits and compulsions.

Acceptance and Commitment Therapy (ACT)

The ACT is a form of psychotherapy that is rooted in the practices of traditional CBT but focuses on action-oriented approaches. The goal of ACT is for patients to stop engaging in behaviors of avoidance, denial, and struggling when it comes to their own inner emotions. Rather than experiencing these behaviors, the patient learns to accept these feelings, recognize them as being appropriate responses to the stimuli that caused them, and commit to continuing to move forward in their lives anyway. The goal here is for them to recognize that what they are feeling is normal and natural and that it does not need to hold them back or prevent them from continuing to move forward in life.

Patients of ACT are taught to accept issues and hardships in their lives and commit to making the necessary changes in their behavior so that they can stop feeling victimized by the experiences they have had. They also have to commit to making these changes in their thoughts, feelings, and emotions. The ACT is highly similar to CBT, except that the focus is more on accepting and committing to moving on, whereas the focus of CBT is identifying and committing to change.

Chapter 11 Cognitive Behavioral Activities and Exercises

Essential Cognitive Behavioral Therapy Techniques and Tools

The beauty of CBT techniques is that they can be used beyond the therapy. A patient can incorporate these techniques into their daily life and fight away from their anxiety disorders.

There are many pills that you can take for anxiety. Unfortunately, these are just temporary reliefs that won't fix the root problem.

There's a chance that by this point, you are already feeling a little bit better. Sometimes, all it takes is sharing and confronting your feelings for you to have a better sense of yourself and the things that trigger you. Telling just one person about trauma, a secret, or something that you fear can make you feel better. Having to keep all that to yourself can cause a lot of strain. That's added responsibility that you might not always have the mental capacity for.

It all starts with identifying your root causes. Is it body image issues from society or your parents? Did you have abusive family members that hurt you physically and mentally? Perhaps it was a great trauma that has led to depression and anxiety in your adult life.

Make sure that you are taking notes on what those are. If something pops into your head, jot it down so you can look back at it later. Remember that you aren't going to be able to unravel it all right away. At first, you might just be able to look back at your life and see the loss of a parent as the root cause of some issues. Once you explore that, you will discover other small instances that experience affected and how that has resulted in the way that you think today.

After you have identified the root cause, you can start to see how it has manifested itself into your life. Do you experience obsessive-compulsive disorder after parental abandonment? Do you have social anxiety because of your body image issues? When we look at the 'what' of our mental illness, we can look at the 'why', and vice versa. Sometimes, you might first notice your habits before the cause, or maybe you already know the employment-related and can now use that to explain your behaviour now. Either way, it is important to make sure that you are aware of this so you can come up with specific cognitive behavioural therapy tools to overcome that.

Now, it is time to start to see what we can do to turn these thoughts and feelings around. Instead of finding a quick fix, we have to look at long-term solutions to help us overcome fear and anxiety. These are all methods that aren't going to solve all your problems right away. They are things that you need to practice, but with time, they become easier. It took a while to develop the automatic thoughts you have now, so you can't expect that they'll stop after reading this book. After a while, however, you will find that they come naturally to you.

Mindfulness

Mindfulness is going to be one of the most helpful tools for all forms of mental illness. Whether you are anxious all the time, or just experience social anxiety in situations with other people around you, you can benefit from mindfulness. It can be helpful for those that have constant depressive thoughts as well.

It can be easy to run away with your thoughts when you are feeling stressed and overwhelmed. You might escape to a place in your mind, real or not, where you don't have to think about the present. It might be a fantasy of a life that's better than the one you are living, or perhaps you often reminisce on times that were better than now.

Mindfulness is the attempt to ground you and keep you in reality, rather than lost in your anxious and stressful thoughts. When you think of one anxious thing, it can easily lead to many other worries. For example, you might think, "Oh no, I have to pay the cable bill because it is already late." Then you might start thinking of all the other bills stacking up, not to mention the debt that's increasing in interest. Then you start to think about how you aren't making enough money at your current job, or that you should have gone to school for a different subject, or you shouldn't have broken up with that guy who's now a doctor. One thought about a late cable bill can lead to an existential crisis if you don't stop anxiety right in its tracks. Mindfulness will help you through this. Instead of ruminating on what could have, would have, or should have been, you instead focus on the now, which is what is most important.

It is something that needs to be practiced. You might only be able to be comfortably mindful for a few seconds at a time before your thoughts go straight back to something else. When you find that you are losing yourself in your thoughts, you have to make sure that you redirect. Back to the example of the cable bill, you might notice your anxiety rising when you think of the other bills stacking up. That is when you would stop your thoughts and instead use a mindful tactic to bring you back to the present and instead focus on the cable bill.

Then, you might find that your mind is wandering again, and before you know it, you are thinking about that wealthy guy and what could have been. You have not failed, but you just need to redirect again, either using a new mindful technique or just practicing the other one again. Don't punish yourself for drifting back into those thoughts.

Picture yourself driving down a highway. The present is the road in front of you, the past the grass to the right, and the future the other road on the left. If you drift too far right or left, then you'll get lost and off track. Mindfulness is what's going to keep you moving forward in the right direction. At first, you are going to be driving down the road very wobbly. Every time you feel yourself drift off to the right or the left, redirect and focus back on going straight. Eventually, you'll find it very easy to avoid drifting at all.

Mindfulness should be practiced whenever you find that you are experiencing symptoms of anxiety. You should practice mindfulness even when you aren't in a negative mindset. Maybe you are just bored or restless, which are also forms of anxiety. We don't always view being bored as a bad thing, and many people feel lucky if they get the chance to have nothing to occupy their time. If you are bored for too long, however, you might find your thoughts drifting somewhere dangerous, so practice mindfulness even if you don't feel like you are that anxious.

Even if you aren't feeling anxious, you can still use these to help prevent future moments of anxiety. No harm will come from mindfulness. These aren't the only methods of mindfulness either.
Some activities would be considered mindful, such as playing a game or reading a book. Anything that keeps your mind on the

present is going to be mindful. We might not always have the time to play a game or read a book to pull us out of our thoughts, however, so it is important to remember to use these tools for when you are feeling anxious.

Five Senses

Your five senses are your ability to see, smell, taste, hear, and touch. When being mindful, a good form is to go through each of these senses to feel better. This activity starts by sitting somewhere comfortably, preferably with your feet flat on the floor. When you are in a comfortable place, it is easier for your mind to focus on what it needs to. You might be feeling anxious at work, waiting at the doctor's office, or just in your own home. No matter where you are, you can go through this process to help ground you and keep you at the moment, avoiding anxious and depressive automatic thoughts.
First is your sight.

Find five things that you can see. This is just simply anything that is in your range of eyesight. It might be the rug that your feet are on or the building you see out the window. Perhaps it is the table with things sitting on them and all the stuff that's on top. Whatever your five items are, it doesn't matter. The only thing you have to do is identify them.

Next, identify four things that you can smell. Don't get up from where you are sitting to employment-related them. Just try to pick them out. Maybe it is the coffee sitting on the counter or a manhole you see walking down the street. Perhaps you imagine smelling the cat, or the candy sitting in the dish on the table.

Look for three things to touch. These are easily identifiable things. It might include the couch you are sitting on, your hair, or your pants. Maybe it is just something across the room, like a salt lamp, or a soft scarf hanging on the coat rack. You don't have to touch these things either. Just think about what three things you could touch.

Find two things you could hear. This could include the birds chirping outside or the music softly playing on the elevator. Perhaps it is the tapping of someone else's foot or the sound of nails scraping on a table. Whatever these are, pick them out.

Pick out one thing that you can taste. This isn't something that has to be edible either. Maybe it is the taste of the water from a fountain in front of you or a sandwich someone else is eating. No matter what it is, everything has a flavour, edible or not, and your goal is just to identify that taste.

You don't have to do these activities. You don't have to taste something or smell something. But identifying it as something that you could use that for can be enough to pull you back into the moment. You don't have to go in that order either. Instead, you can try finding five things to touch, four things to hear, three things to taste, two things to smell, and one thing to see. Just remember your five senses and a descending amount.

If you don't have one of these senses, such as the ability to hear, see, or taste, then simply replace that with another sense. Either way, the goal is to give you something you can identify at the moment so that you are pulled away from the anxious thoughts in the first place.

Finding Colours

Another activity for mindfulness is to search for one specific colour. When you are feeling anxious, think of one colour. It shouldn't be something specific at first, just simply pick something like blue, black, grey, white, or yellow.
Look around the room and pick out everything that is that colour. This doesn't have to be done in any specific order. Simply look for red things, or green, or any other simple colour. Again, if you don't have this ability and are colour

blind, try using a different "rule." Maybe you find only things that are made of metal, or you pick out all the things made of wood.

Identify what might be a close sister of that colour. After picking out all the green stuff, look at that specifically and think about what's lime green, what's forest green, and everything in between.

Before you know it, your mind is on something completely different than what was making you anxious. There are no rules for this either. If you miss an item, nothing bad will happen. The goal is to get your brain to stop thinking about what's causing anxiety and instead look directly toward what's around you at the current moment.

If it isn't working at first, try repeating with a different colour. Do this after you do the five senses or vice versa. Come up with your games too, like identifying all the things that make white noise, or the things that you can smell that are made of wood. The only thing you have to make sure you are doing is that you are focusing on the now and not on the past or future.

Muscle Relaxation

When we're anxious, it can be hard to realize just how much we might be using our muscles. Your back, jaw, neck, shoulders, and other parts of your body that are responsible for support can be sore often if you don't properly manage your anxiety. There are even some people that believe certain pains are associated with certain issues, such as lower back and hip pain being caused by money issues. This isn't proven by science, but it is interesting to think about just how much pain we might be feeling simply because of our anxiety.

Tensing and releasing your muscles is a good form of mindfulness that keeps you focused on the now, and that will help your body feel better afterward too. It involves identifying your muscles and tensing them for three to five seconds and then holding for one to two seconds in between, focusing on deep breathing the entire time. Don't push yourself if it is too straining, and skip over any muscles that might be sore or parts of your body with too much nerve damage. The point isn't to strain yourself, but to focus instead on how tense you are and how to relieve that tension.

Start with your head. Clench your jaw for a few seconds and then release. Raise your ears and hold them tight or tilt your neck to each side for a few seconds. Move down to your shoulders, raising them as high as possible and then dropping them as much as you can. Just when you think you have relaxed your shoulders, relax them even more.

Now, move onto your chest and arms. Hold them tight for a few seconds, releasing for a few afterward. The entire time, make sure that you are fully breathing in and out so that you don't lose your breath. Then, go to your stomach, legs, feet, and repeat if you need to. It is not supposed to be a workout, but just a way for you to become aware of how tense you might be. Our muscles can become very sore if we don't properly hold them right.

Between each of these muscle tightening moments, make sure to take a deep breath in and let it out slowly. Count your breathing and count how long you are holding. Consistency will help regulate your heart and lungs so that those too help with overall anxiety reduction.

This is why exercising can be so relaxing for many people. It gets your mind focused on something else and also keeps the blood pumping. Remember that exercise is healthy and important, but it can also be a source of anxiety. Don't put pressure on yourself to be physical right away, especially if that's one of your triggers. The gym can be a scary place, and even walking down the street can cause people to panic, so while it is important to keep your body moving to avoid anxious symptoms, don't make yourself feel bad that you aren't in a place where you can do this.

Journaling

This is one of the best techniques for treating anxiety disorders. It allows one to be able to evaluate the things that are happening around him. There are a lot of things taking place at any given time if you are careful enough to take notice. Journaling is the art of documenting your life. It helps you make sense of the decisions that you take and it also helps you understand what's ailing you. In the case of a person who's struggling with anxiety disorder, taking stock of the various undesirable things that are happening in your life, you'd be in a better position to get rid of your anxieties and become a well-adjusted person. In the modern era, there is much physical and mental stimulation thanks to technological advancement. So, ensure that you record all the activities you have gotten into, all the significant thoughts you have, as well as negative emotions. It is not realistic to record every single event or emotion but you can stick to the important things. When you have the habit of journaling your day and thoughts you will be in a better position to manage your anxiety and improve the quality of your life.

Understand your cognitive distortions

In almost every case of chronic anxiety, the victim holds at least a flawed perception. But the CBT practitioner helps them look at all their beliefs and thought patterns in a given order they might be able to identify their distorted perceptions. At the heart of many fears and anxieties is an inability to have an accurate idea of what's going on in reality. And so, the person is driven to act in a manner that is considered unbecoming. To understand one's cognitive distortions, they need to look at their lives critically and interrogate the decisions that they have made. Also, it's important to be honest with yourself because one might easily justify their actions or thoughts.

Restructuring of cognitive distortions

Once you identify cognitive distortions you have to take it a notch further by restructuring these cognitive distortions so that you might become well-adjusted. With the help of the CBT practitioner, you should interrogate how you came to develop a certain distorted belief. For instance, if your body image has been so negative that you have developed chronic anxiety off of thinking about how you look, you start by pointing out your cognitive distortions, which might be: emotional reasoning and overgeneralizations.

Once you identify these cognitive distortions you must take a step further and interrogate how they came to take firm root within you. In the case of emotional reasoning, maybe you have always "felt" as though people were judging your body weight or shape or skin. And you tended to make decisions depending on your emotional state. The practitioner helps you understand that there's no direct link between what your emotions tell you and the reality.

For instance, if your emotions tell you that people hate you, people are against you, it is not necessarily true. People can only hate you if you have been nasty on them. They can't simply hate you for existing near them.

The CBT practitioner helps you understand how you came to cling onto these misleading and distorted perceptions of reality. One of the accelerators for the development of cognitive distortions is low self-esteem. A person with low self-esteem is bound to think themselves unworthy of success and they are highly likely to exhibit self-inhibiting tendencies.

Their mental instability makes them prime targets for cognitive distortions.

Restructuring these cognitive distortions is the first major step towards overcoming anxieties and leading a well-adjusted life.

Exposure technique

Assuming that your anxiety is spurred into life by an event, you can remedy this problem by confronting your fears, as opposed to running away from them. For instance, if you become a nervous wreck every time you come close to members of the opposite sex, ensure that you put yourself in more situations that force you to talk with members of the opposite sex.

Once you have talked to enough members of the opposite sex you will start to feel less anxious and with the time you will become confident around them. It might seem quite easy on text but in real life it's hard.

This is an event that has always caused you anxiety, so in your mind, it will be a seemingly insurmountable mountain. Set for yourself both short term and long term goals to ensure that you overcome your anxiety. You can start by meeting one or two members of the opposite sex, and as your confidence goes up, you may increase the number of people you meet. Focus not only on the meeting but ensuring that you have a good discussion going. As you perform all these exercises, your subconscious mind is watching, and it will assist you in developing solid confidence around members of the opposite sex.

Finish the script

Think of anything that fills you up with fear and makes you anxious. The reason why you give off such a strong reaction is because your mind is fixated on the possible outcome, but if you were brave enough to stick through, you would realize that nothing would come of it. For instance, if you tend thinking obsessively about your troubling past, you might try to suppress these thoughts hoping that your anxiety will go away. Now, instead of suppressing these emotions you should keep poring over them. This will send a message to your subconscious mind that you are not scared of the matter anymore and you will realize that nothing happens.

It can be a daunting task to let your fear-filled thoughts play out through your mind's eye. But then it's all a matter of practicing. The more you practice to exert control on your thoughts, the more you are in control of your thoughts and behaviours. Letting your fearful thoughts play out and ultimately realizing that they pose no serious threat can be an incredibly freeing moment as it becomes apparent that your anxiety is fuelled by a non-real threat.

The CBT practitioner plays a critical role in guiding the patient to entertain a certain thought and stick to it so that they may finally realize that they don't have reason to be anxious.

Diaphragmatic breathing

This is another awesome method of fighting away anxiety. Some people seem not to understand how an involuntary exercise – breathing – can be said to help fight off anxiety. But what they fail to consider is the fact that diaphragmatic breathing is voluntary. And also, that it is not as easy as they might think. If you perform this exercise as it should be done, you will find it extremely challenging.

Ensure that you are in a serene environment. Then take your favorite spot (either lying standing or sitting) and then close your eyes and put your hand on your stomach. Slowly, you may draw air in through your nose and then expel it through your mouth. You will notice that with every breath your diaphragm will expand.

As you breathe out, ensure that you imaginatively cast away your ill thoughts. This will help a great deal in getting rid of anxieties. So precisely how do deep breathing exercises help alleviate anxieties?

A relaxed state of being: Deep breathing exercises will help you get into a state of relaxation. You will cease to feel the pressures. And such a mental state doesn't encourage the development of anxieties.

Lowers heartbeat: Apart from fighting off your anxious nature, deep breathing exercises will also help lower your rate of heartbeat. As you may know, having an extremely high rate of heartbeat might put you at risk of developing heart health issues.

Helps you deal with post-traumatic stress disorder: Some people have anxiety that arises from their post-traumatic stress disorder. One of the ways of overcoming the negative thinking patterns induced by PTSD is through performing deep breathing exercises. They help you calm down and get into a great headspace.

Promotes thought clarity: Sometimes we put ourselves into trouble because of our inability to think matters through. So, what would happen if we had it in us to hold clear thoughts? We would be in a position to make the best decisions and save ourselves the problem of anxieties.

Engaging in deep breathing exercises is one of the best ways to increase our mental alertness and ensure that we have mental clarity. This helps us make good decisions.

Chapter 12 How to Prevent Depression

Nothing changes for you if you don't take the first step. Making up your mind to stand up to whatever is holding you back is when you will truly make progress. If you are on medications for anxiety and doing every other thing there is to get better; it won't make a real difference until you practice self-care yourself.

Anxiety disorder is not as simple as a single feeling of being on edge. It is a culmination of different factors that make a person behaves the way they do.

What is Mindfulness?

Like the word itself, it means the mind is only occupied with what is happening in the present. The mind's main focus is on what is happening in the space you are occupying and the present task at hand. This seems like a minor thing to have such a fuss about but it is important. There are so many people other than those with anxiety who can't seem to focus or concentrate on the present. Usually, the mind veers to the future or the past. This is the root cause of anxiety and panic attacks.

Mindfulness can make us snap to reality no matter where our mind diverges to. Mindfulness is an innate ability that some have mastered more than others. It is not a new skill or discovery. It makes people better equipped to pay attention and enable them to stay more focused than others. You can also learn to hone this natural ability. It can prove to be significant for anyone. Using mindfulness to beat the panic is one of the most effective methods. Some of the methods to improve your mindfulness are through different techniques of meditation. Some of which are:

- Lying down

- Walking

- Being seated

Mindfulness is different for everyone. It doesn't mean that a bunch of people who practice it more consciously become more alike in personality. Mindfulness can make you become more of who you already are.

Mindfulness is guaranteed to improve your relationships, and have a positive impact on work and health. Life can be more meaningful without the unnecessary stress. You will be able to see things more clearly and respond better. Simply put, it will make your lifestyle more efficient. You will be able to approach your daily experiences with open-mindedness and be gentler toward yourself too.

Benefits of Mindfulness

- Some of the benefits of mindfulness:

- Improve sleep quality. You will see results just after a little while of practicing; it will boost your body's immune system.

- It will directly reduce anxiety and stress. It is a sure way to increase positive emotions that will help you prevent relapsing from stress.

- It can increase gray matter in some of our brain areas that are: empathy, memory, learning, and emotional regulation. So, that means you can get better in all of those things by just practicing mindfulness.

- Mindfulness will let us stop worrying about unnecessary things, so we get a chance to see the real picture. It can lead to one being more altruistic and compassionate not only to others but to themselves also.

- One of the things anxiety chips away from us is our self-esteem and confidence. Mindfulness can help you regain that and build a much more positive image of yourself. You are then more likely to act on your values.

- It can also help in dealing with past trauma. Since mindfulness means to survive in the now, you will become more resilient about your past. It can help with anxiety disorders that stem from past experiences.

- Mindfulness can help you in every walk of life. It can help you with decision making and increasing creativity. These two things combined spell progress in your workplace.

- It will reduce stress for parents so they would pay better attention to their kids. In schools, it has very effective and positive results for students. Teaching kids' mindfulness can help them with behavior problems and aggression.

Mindfulness practices:

Meditation is a practice that has numerous mental health benefits despite seemingly being a simple thing. We gain more awareness and insight through it. It can notably help to reduce stress and increase productiveness. Mindfulness will suspend the judgment element of your brain and you get to focus on other things.

Mindfulness has several factors:

- Pay attention to your senses at the moment. Otherwise, you would miss their signals and easily let your mind wander.

- In case of experiencing an overwhelming panic attack, pay attention to your breathing.

- Throughout the day, reserve some moments for practicing mindfulness. It will help you clear your head and focus more.

- Drilling positive thought patterns into your brain consist of recognizing that our thoughts and emotions are not bigger than us. They do not define us.

Here are several exercises that will help you acquire the necessary mindfulness skills.

Raisin Exercise

You are to utilize each of your senses, one by one, to pay attention to a raisin. For example, the feel of it by your hands or its smell. It will help you practice more to be at the moment.

Walking

It is a daily activity that has brought more value to, by paying attention to it. You are to focus on the movement of your feet touching and leaving the ground.

Mindful Breathing

As breath goes in and out, you are told to practice to focus on the physical sensations you feel.

Build Compassion through Mindfulness

This kind of meditation is focused on compassion towards others and more importantly to yourself. The first step is to practice it towards you then slowly to your closed ones. It goes off like that then finally to people you don't care about or have a negative feeling about them.

Mindfulness and Anxiety

Life happens to you as it does to everybody. It is not always the case of liking life but we always like to make it responsible whenever something bad happens. We should be open to experiencing good and bad aspects of life by taking them as they are.

Anxiety is part of being human. So many people experience it on the regular. It has not been recognized as a disorder.

Mindfulness-based therapies are solely about the relationship between the person experiencing anxiety and their thoughts. The relationship is not great, to say the least hence the anxiety, so mindfulness is there to try and change that.

A person is made aware and to confront the bodily sensations that come along whenever he or she is feeling anxiety. They are made to fully experience what goes on at that moment rather than trying to hide from it like they have been doing before. The withdrawing was not working and it never does in case of anxiety. So, it is better to buckle up and face the music. It is not only the physical symptoms they are made to face but also their thoughts. They are advised to open up to them. Experiencing all these thoughts will eventually make a person realize that they were not true, to begin with. They have been avoiding them for no reason and building up their anxiety about them.

The person practicing mindfulness will be taught to realize and respond to their distressing thoughts and then they will start letting them go. Not acknowledging them was the problem in the first place.

Breath-Control

Your breathing tends to become shallower as you panic more. So, if you start experiencing panic then immediately start counting your breaths while keeping your eyes closed. If your breathing has turned rapid then just focus on a couple of inhales and exhales. While counting, if your mind is not focused on breathing, then it means success. You have practiced mindfulness in a trying time.

Become Aware of your Body

When experiencing a panic attack, try to pay attention to your body and what is happening to every part of it. Try to feel your toes and fingers and sense if your muscles are tensing up. As you become aware of this feeling, try to let it happen and do not try to resist it. Just becoming aware will help you but resisting will make it worse.

Become Aware of your Surrounding

It is not always the case that keeping to your eyes while having a panic attack will help you resist it. More often than not, being aware of your surroundings helps more. So, open your eyes and try to interact with your surroundings via your brain. Say hello to things present in your room. It will help you ground yourself.

By experiencing a nervous or stressful situation, an anxious person reacts to it which is usually via an unnecessary fight or flight response. It has no business in the majority of situations an anxious person is involved in. Thus, by mindfulness instead of reacting, you are taught to respond to them positively. It is done by practicing to be present in your body and fully knowing what is going on that is giving you anxiety in the first place. You will eventually figure out it was all about a thing that you are perceiving and categorizing as threats. As you will find anxiety to be nothing more than a perceived threat, it will vanish on its own.

Mindfulness-based therapies are proved to be helpful in reducing depression.

Some people find it impossible to just sit still for a while. Meditation involves staying still and could be a very daunting task for them. A worthwhile solution for them is to take a pause during the day and just take five deep breaths. That should do it for them. You can practice it whenever you feel.

Sometimes it helps to practice mindfulness with a group of people. You will see you are not an outlier and everyone makes mistakes. That will help you stick to mindfulness and not to give up on it. Meditation is thought of as a solo activity, but more often than not it helps to do it while being part of a group.

Some people even have heightened anxiety when trying to sit still and meditate. It is advisable to let it pass and not let your determination waver. It is the key if you want to bring a positive change in your life.

The distressing thoughts that you are so afraid to face, once you let them pass without reacting, you will gain a new skillset. One that will next time guide you on how to deal with fear and anxious thoughts.

Mindfulness can make you see things more clearly. It will help you achieve inner peace.

Conclusion

Getting through life with a mental illness isn't always easy, whether it is a major depressive disorder, general anxiety disorder, social anxiety disorder, obsessive-compulsive disorder, or anyone of many other disorders. However, with cognitive-behavioral therapy, you can transform a painful and torturous life into a joyful and fulfilled life. No longer do you have to simply push through all of the negative emotions and experiences brought on through your disorder. Instead, you can transform your life with a few simple techniques and hard work.

Cognitive-behavioral therapy will take time, you can expect it to take twelve or more weeks to experience the full benefit, but it is well worth it. Studies have regularly shown that CBT is one of the most effective treatment options for both depression and anxiety, with the longest-lasting results. Medication is rarely enough on its own to control these disorders, but with the addition of CBT, you can keep your mental health in check and prevent relapses.

Before you began this book, you were likely unsure, afraid, and at your wit's end. Yet, you now have all the answers you need to regain your mental health and take control of your life. You can begin to enjoy life, smile, and laugh again, no longer having depressing and anxious thoughts control your every move. All you have to do is begin. Don't wait. Begin week one now, and in twelve short weeks, you will be in a better place. You can be happy again. You can feel like yourself again.

To define depression we would have to look at it from two angles, its minor expression, and its major expression. You won't be wrong to define depression as just having a low spirit. This, however, would be considered as the mildest definition you can give to depression. This definition explains depression as a condition that tends to make life a lot harder for you than it should be with a high spirit. The individual may lead a normal life but will be doing that in a lot harder way than it should be. Life stresses you out because you go through life with less enthusiasm and confidence.

In its major expression, which is considered clinical depression, you can define depression as a life-threatening emotional and psychological condition. In this expression, he depressed individual loses hope and as you already know, hope is one of the driving forces of life in any human. Once hope is lost, life itself gradually fades. The will to do anything at all is lost and nothing matters anymore. At this point, a depressed individual may not only give up on life at all, but the individual may also become suicidal. This is why clinical depression is considered a major cause of depression.

Individuals in this category need special attention after surviving this stage of depression. Clinical depression is a way of putting the entire body system in danger. The whole body gradually shuts down as the body, spirit and should give up on life. Mistakes are repeated, the individual isolates himself from the rest of society. You can consider clinical depression as a mood disorder that is defined by an almost loss of the zeal to go through a lie or pursue any o life's pleasure or you can simply define it as a heavily depressed mood.

There are different types of depression and they are based on their unique effects on the patient. Some of them are named according to their causes.

People often make the mistake of concluding that those who are depressed or those going through clinical depression and have attempted suicide are weak. Depression as a health condition is not easy to deal with by the individual alone and most times the individual needs the support of loved ones and a professional to get through it.

The only time anxiety becomes entirely bad is when it interferes completely with your daily life and affects your sense of judgment. When you are no longer able to make rational decisions and become prone to making mistakes, then, it becomes a problem. When anxiety becomes an everyday response, when it becomes overwhelming, you need to have yourself checked. When fear and worries due to anxiety interfere with your relationships and ultimately affects your daily life negatively—it is only wise to assume at that point that it is no longer normal anxiety. You have most likely drift into an anxiety disorder. One thing about anxiety disorders is that they are a group of related conditions rather than a single disorder this is why symptoms may often differ from one person to another. Because of this, you must go check-up with a professional before concluding that an individual has an anxiety disorder. You cannot use a person's anxiety symptoms to diagnose another person of anxiety disorder. We all have our natural responses to the things around us and as a matter of fact, different people will respond differently to the same condition in the same place and at the same time. This is why it will be wrong to use one person's symptom as a yardstick for diagnosing another person of the same health condition. There may be similarities in their responses, but it doesn't mean they have the same condition. This is exactly the case with anxiety.